MW00988401

SEMIOTEXT(E) INTERVENTION SERIES

Original title: *La Droitisation du monde*
© Éditions Textuel, 2016. 13 Quai de Conti, 75006 Paris.
www.editionstextuel.com
This translation © 2018 by Semiotext(e).

Published by Semiotext(e)
PO BOX 629, South Pasadena, CA 91031
www.semiotexte.com

Special thanks to Robert Dewhurst.

Design: Hedi El Kholti

ISBN: 978-1-63590-016-3
Distributed by The MIT Press, Cambridge, Mass.
and London, England
Printed in the United States of America

François Cusset

How the World Swung

to the Right

Fifty Years of Counterrevolutions

Translated by Noura Wedell

semiotext(e)
intervention
series □ 25

Contents

Introduction

Two thousand seventeen. Donald Trump inaugurates his presidency by restricting Muslims' access to the United States. He raises the value-added tax on Mexican imports to compel Mexico to pay for the giant wall he wants to build along its border, touts his contempt for environmental protections, asserts lies and provocations as legitimate modes of governance, and in the very first days of his term labels the American press the "great enemy of the people." Rodrigo Duterte, president of the Philippines, boasts of slaughtering ghetto "drug scum" and incites vigilantes to kill thousands of drug users and small dealers. He goes so far as to call Pope Francis a "son of a whore" after the pope expressed concern about the killings. Corrupt governments in Latin America and in Africa, when they aren't brought to justice or toppled by political opponents, instantly flout the electors who brought them to power, and silence legal opposition as much as they can. The Syrian dictator Bachar-al-Assad continues to bomb and gas his own people, as he has done for the last six years. Iran is unwilling to loosen its conservative grip. In this second decade of the new millennium, international models of geopolitical stability and macroeconomic efficacy include the following: an ultranationalist and autocratic Turkey, with Recep Tayyip Erdoğan implicitly accepting as a compliment the label of "dictator" given him by the West; Vladimir Putin's autocratic and Islamophobic Russia; the Wahhabi monarchy's neofeudal Saudi Arabia; and, despite slowing growth, a record-breaking China, which is more than ever indifferent to the question of public freedom.[1] Europe, which is supposedly more "unified" than anywhere, is undergoing an unprecedented crisis of representative democracy. The temptations of populism and extreme-right nationalisms are on the rise. This has spurred the British to leave Europe. It has encouraged the Hungarians to allow their xenophobic leader Viktor Orbán to censor them. Like other leaders of former Eastern Bloc countries, he is launching an aggressive campaign to expel foreign NGOs. This wave of nationalism has also compelled Germans to dissuade their dear chancellor from welcoming more Syrian refugees, and in its wake the French have made Marine Le

Pen's National Front the primary political power in the nation, or at least the last one that can still stir up true enthusiasm. But only half a century ago, and more or less successfully, all of these countries were driven by radically different agendas. They were fighting for civil rights and for the welfare state. They were led by the secularism of Mustapha Kemal Atatürk, by secular pan-Arabism, and by postcolonial progressism. There was hope, after Roosevelt, for a "new frontier." Or, much more cruelly, countries were under the sway of Mao Zedong and Nikita Khrushchev's authoritarian communisms. In a little over forty years, the world has fallen under a new threefold rule. It is headed by volatile financial markets and uncontrolled multinationals or by partisans of nationalist and/or religious withdrawal, and heads of states are a new (or perhaps not so new) species of dictator and wink at each other from all parts of the globe and claim that they are ready to welcome the newcomer Trump as one of their own.[2] How did this happen?

Let's try to explain how we got here. Beyond listing a few proper names, or describing a few nightmarish heads of state, let's try to understand what ideological, cultural, and socioeconomic seeds have yielded such rotten fruit. This is where it gets complicated. Fifty years ago, people in the political, cultural, and activist worlds were thinking in a radically different way—if someone who had been frozen in the 1960s woke up today, they would not understand anything about the contemporary world, despite the fact that its general coordinates seem to have remained the same. There are still cities, jobs, hurried commuters, vehicles and roads, and different kinds of knowledge and power. But if this time traveler had been concerned with social progress, with artistic creation, or with collective desire, they would not find anything meaningful today. Our world would be largely incomprehensible. And if ever they had been concerned about the political division between the Right and the Left, they would have a hard time recognizing those two categories in the contemporary world, and their knowledge of them would now be useless. We have perhaps entered an era in which the very word "left" has become useless, obscure, embarrassing. In fact, we might just have to do without it.

If we look at the usage of the term "left," it's striking to note that today's most interesting or determined social movements barely use it at all. "Left" is mostly cast aside, although the term "emancipation" sometimes serves as a vague rubric for the different experiences coming under its orbit. A few movements (in Latin America, for example) use the term "on the left" to define themselves. However, beyond instituted parties that use it sparingly, the term does not seem necessary to the new generations of activists. Take the secularized and social Islam of the 2011 Arab Spring uprisings, or the "occupiers" of North American and Southern European public squares that same year, or what appeared in France in April 2016 around the Nuit Debout movement. None of these movements used the term "left." It has become useless and heavy. The media, on the other hand, still use it on a large scale when they comment on the parties and programs that are officially in power. Paradoxically, it is as if the term pointed to the fact that officially "socialist" or proudly social-democratic governments were no longer on the left, or were betraying the values that had previously been associated with the term. Opposite them—where an ancient leftist, emancipatory, and equalitarian tradition is reinventing itself in the streets and in a concrete utopia—the term "left" is barely used.

It's true that the young rebels of the 1960s did not always describe themselves as "on the left," but the period was much more strict and dogmatic ideologically. The term "left" was less present than were its doctrinal variants—Marxism, Leninism, Situationism, Maoism, etc. For everyone, from actors and adversaries to observers, these were possible contemporary forms of the idea of "the Left." The idea was still alive, as it had been transmitted through the social struggles of the nineteenth century, from the Belgian miners to the female workers of the Laurence Mills, from the New Deal to the Popular Front and the Marxist revolutions of the twentieth century. A historical continuity was still inscribed in the very idea of "the Left." Today, however, no one mentions that anymore. The word is only faintly whispered by some, or pronounced with a twinge of shame. After all, it seems that the left/right polarity has become perfectly artificial. It was born with the first revolutionary assembly of 1789 in Paris, where the arbitrary nature of a single chamber suddenly designated as "the Right" those who were seated to the right of the rostrum, whereas the Girondins, the Montagnards, and the antiroyalists were on the left. This rhetorical convention has had two centuries of rich history, but we can very well let it go.

The more serious question concerns the doctrinal and programmatic content of the terms "right" and "left," and their relevance today. On my end, the only reason to keep the term "left" is if it maintains one fundamental meaning, a meaning that is more vague than its doctrinal content but sharper than debates in the chamber: that is, the sense of *conflict*. "Left" implies an antagonistic position, a power of resistance, and a very general sense of counterhegemony in action.

Hegemony today is maintained through conservative values, the entrenchment of norms, the exclusion of minorities, and via the chaotic triumph of neoliberal capitalism. If all we maintain in the use of the term "left" is this very general sense of active counterhegemony, we are also taking the risk of removing or modifying its precise historical ingredients: statism, social justice, hospitality, and the redistribution of wealth. But those notions have themselves evolved. To take a simple example, the social equality traditionally defined by the socialist project did not take into account sexual domination, or the postcolonial question, or the question of invisible and unheard minorities. If we want to integrate those issues, which are crucial contemporary questions today, we can no longer keep the same doctrinal content for the old term "left." To stop the unfortunate cycle of recent decades, we must reinvent everything.

1

A COUNTERREVOLUTION IN THREE PARTS

1. The Origins of the Contemporary Disaster

Throughout the world, an immense shift to the right has taken place. It is based on a double historical assessment. First, since the early 1970s, the world has shifted massively to the right through many, often contradictory forms. Among these we can list the end of the so-called real communisms, the dislocation of the welfare state, the privatization and commodification of all sectors of society, the financialization of the economy, the extension of the supposedly benevolent control of "life," the turn toward security policies in international relations, the excessive policing of social relations and the control of all by all, a cultural and religious backlash under the fallacious pretense of a "clash" of civilizations, a rise in nationalist nostalgias, and the criminalization and the individualization of modes of life and behavior. To put it bluntly, this didn't start with Donald Trump; he simply came along at the right time to harvest what *we* all had sown … But secondly, in the shorter term—that is, over the last ten years—we've seen the collective refusal of this state of affairs, a refusal that is still heterogeneous and fueled by many different causes, yet is expressed and organized on a large scale. This is the beginning of a series of uprisings (such as those that led to the overthrow of dictatorships during the Arab Spring) and new social movements in the West, whose chances of success in the short term still seem quite slim. And yet, statistically, the pace and frequency of popular uprisings throughout the world have risen spectacularly in the last twelve years. This is attested to by the tracking tool that the anthropologist Alain Bertho has developed to monitor international riots and uprisings via mainstream news outlets, regional news agencies, and police sources.[1]

Some will say that social instability is difficult to define objectively, and that a single negligible event can trigger major upheavals while huge riots can have no effect. However, if direct confrontations with the forces of law and order on a large scale and over an extended period of time lead on both sides to physical damages, arrests, and incarcerations, there will be objective and measurable data. Of course, the effect of a revolt depends to a large extent on its context, what Lenin used to call "objective circumstances." There are historical circumstances in which the mysterious death of a young boy from the hood after a cop chase can simply lead to a bereaved family; there are others in which this same event can ignite the neighborhood for months on end. This is why these events should be viewed as symptoms of a certain situation—as signs of a world, and not its cause.

What is clear is that the long era from the early 1980s to the mid-2000s, during which social mobilization was in decline, seems to be ending on a global scale. During this time uprisings and protests were either sporadic and contained by those in power, or linked to specific wars. The new era replacing it is still quite difficult to qualify. Now, popular uprisings last longer, are more frequent, and are more widespread throughout the globe. Beyond its varied forms and causes, this new era emerges from a collective reaction to what is felt to be the fourfold disaster of the contemporary world: the *social, economic, geopolitical,* and *environmental* disaster. On the social front, following a century and a half of a system of partial redistribution associated with the progressive institution of the welfare state, the emperor now has new clothes. The so-called developing countries are planning their development without a welfare apparatus, whereas the more developed countries are allowing huge pockets of poverty to grow in their midst. In terms of economics, globalized and financialized neoliberal capitalism is no longer forced to play the game of regulation. Authorities, institutional safeguards, and systemic countereffects can no longer contain its excesses. On the political front, the so-called democratic states are playing it by ear in the face of a degree of discredit and a level of abstention that is without precedent in the last fifty years. These states operate as optimization consultants for the great market, daily management services for an economic order that makes all decisions for them. This is how we should understand Donald Trump's election; he is less a xenophobic clown or a reality-TV conspirator than the cynical CEO of the conglomerate Amerika, Inc. Finally, on the environmental level, the very existence of life on earth is now endangered in the foreseeable future, at least if we extend our current macroeconomic growth curves. Faced with our quadruple disaster, spontaneous forms of day-to-day resistance as well as popular revolts have recently emerged. Although they are more emancipatory than identitarian, these struggles are neither on the left nor on the right, and are therefore liable to be seized upon by all the new populisms, or even to be directed toward the cultural, ethnic, and religious conflicts that are tearing apart certain regions of the globe.

Let us review the stages of what amounts to a five-decade long continuous slippage to the right, and let us examine the diabolical coherence of a dogged transformation that was deployed so quickly, without hesitation or pause. To begin with, is "the Right" an adequate term for a phenomenon whose content has varied so greatly since the 1980s? It seems that the fairly coherent term "neoliberalism" more precisely designates the collection of discourses and practices seeking to apply the norms and objectives of the market to social, cultural, and individual life. Yet the term remains somewhat vague, and has been mainly associated with the return of a doctrinal conservatism that was absent from the initial neoliberal program. A cursory history of this shift reminds us that fifty years ago, in the mid 1960s, the world was committed to a very different program, and engaged in emancipation on a global scale. From the 1940s to the late 1960s, half of the known world decolonized. There were a plethora of social and countercultural movements, notably youth uprisings and civil rights struggles in the West. Provisions were made for redistributive and mixed-economy welfare states. Finally, in the Eastern Bloc, the first fault lines appeared around the struggle for the defense of civil liberties, even if these movements were stillborn: the Prague Spring, Tito's Yugoslavia, Budapest in 1956, etc.

Many have insisted on countercultural movements as emblems of this period. These followed the logic of previous artistic elites, and would end up in the "underground" when they did not disappear completely. One of the most reliable signs that this was an emancipatory period was the fact that cultural production was inseparable from a political project and a social collective. This is to say that cultural production adhered to the simplest definition of the avant-garde, in which art and culture are at the forefront of a sociopolitical (r)evolution that steers them and gives them meaning. Indeed, the great cultural avant-gardes of the twentieth century, from the surrealists to the Situationists, shared that higher goal as well as the related refusal to be interested in art or culture *as such*—and never ruled out that art could disappear or sacrifice itself in light of a political revolution or a metamorphosis of daily life. They fetishized their own practices very little, and made sure that they were associated with alternative forms of life and with a comprehensive revolutionary project: to change life, love, language, beauty, and social relations. In contrast, during the succeeding period—that half-century of counterrevolutions that we are emerging from with great difficulty—culture detached itself from collective forms of life and from a social project. Culture became, on the one hand, the most thriving industry of the new capitalism, if not its laboratory of ideas; and, on the other, a collection of devices and situations that were mostly disconnected from the social and political field, a kind of consoling refuge cut off from the exterior world. We could be entertained there, or depressed, but at any rate we'd survive the disaster. Take, for example, the sublime forms of melancholy, catharsis, and self-sufficient and largely fictional counterworlds that appeared throughout this period—or at least at its beginning, in the punk movement of the 1970s and 1980s, in the renewal of science fiction around "cyberpunk" literature and the first video games, in a certain auteur cinema, or simply in the rebellious forms of grunge and hip-hop in the 1990s. The provocations of the Sex Pistols, the punk dandyism of nights at the Palace in Paris or at Studio 54 in New York, Bruce Sterling or William Gibson's pioneering books, Emir Kusturica or David Cronenberg's films, even the fleeting experimentations of the bands Nirvana or Assassin, or the first songs of Afrika Bambaataa … These were all facets of a culture that certainly did not compromise, but that was equally without an outside, a rebellious but antisocial culture, a genuine substitute world for a time that had been abandoned by Progress.

If we go back further in time, we should remember that the political revolution which had inspired the rebellious cycle of the 1960s but which rapidly became impossible lasted for ten to fifteen years longer in the cultural field. It continued, more specifically, in a few marginal countercultural worlds that were symbolically autonomous but disillusioned. Because, indeed, what followed the turbulent era of inseparable cultural creation and social change was the much longer era of global neoliberalization, which dismantled or prohibited the dreams and impulses that had come before it. The new era thus began in the 1970s, quietly at first with misunderstood events such as the military coup led by General Pinochet in Chile in 1973. This event was less the brutal arrival of one more military regime, than it was a political and economic laboratory through which to experiment with brutal deregulation without any claims to democracy. This great premiere had been willed (and supported) by the neoliberal elites who were still a minority among the Western ruling classes. It was also a strategy on the part of the American Secret Service to end a democratic, progressive experiment that was very close to succeeding. With Pinochet replacing Salvador Allende and the latter's pacifist (and so brief) experience of democratic socialism, the United States now had a secure political and economic ally in the region, which would allow them to break the nascent social momentum in

South America. During that same decade, the final repression of Western revolutionary movements that had been running out of steam, a few discreet measures announcing a decisive evolution of the world economy (e.g., the end of the gold standard in 1971), and the emergence in the public sphere of a new genre of ideas and ideologues (e.g., anticommunists and antistatists speaking in the name of market emancipation, moralists and arrogant defenders of the new "antitotalitarian" *doxa* …) were all signaling an imminent shift.

To give a more precise periodization (despite the fact that all periodization is of course arbitrary), we can identify three moments in this vast global shift to the right. Although classification by decades is quite conventional, we can nonetheless distinguish three separate decades, ranging from the first phase of early positioning at the end of the 1970s to our contemporary moment of political radicalization and social resurgence. Each of these decades—the 1980s, 1990s, and 2000s—forms a distinct era. The first was a time of political and ideological takeover that imposed a dual neoliberal and neoconservative agenda in the West, and then in the rest of the world. The second was a moment of doctrinal euphoria, just after the fall of "real" communism, with the toppling of the Berlin Wall and the dismantling of the Soviet Union. This was also the operative phase during which capitalist deregulation and financial globalization were implemented. The third was a decade of ideological opportunism, with neoliberalism—if we can use a single term to refer to something that is so plastic and elastic—in turn choosing strategies of militarization and renationalization in opposition to the principles of its founding fathers, such as Friedrich Hayek, who had always rejected the state in all of its guises, its army and social programs alike. In the 2000s, renationalization became a fact. It occurred first for military reasons, after the attacks of September 11, 2001 and the impossible "War on Terror" launched by George W. Bush with America's occupation of Iraq and Afghanistan and the inauguration of a perpetual political and juridical "state of exception." Renationalization was then prolonged for economic reasons, when the subprime crisis of 2008 incited states to bail out investment banks and insurance companies by means of the most important public fundraising in modern history. In other words, since 9/11 the state has gone back to being modern capitalism's best friend and crucial ally (if ever it had stopped), notably due to the nationalization of losses. This last phase also involved increased repression of protests and the generalization of securitarian control.

On a strictly ideological level, neoliberalism in the 1980s ran on the element of surprise and on doctrinal paradox, establishing a politics of substitution, even a default utopia of the market and of its magic. Competition was "freeing," business creation was "fulfilling," and growth "brought people together." With the neoliberalism of the 1990s came a change in tone. The language was more consensual, more normalizing, and, for lack of legible alternatives, constantly wielded the lie of good intentions and political virtue. Its formula for blackmail was the well-known "if you want democracy you have to have the market." As for neoliberalism in the 2000s, it no longer said anything coherent or doctrinal, but seemed instead to project itself against the ideologies of the previous decades. Chinese, Saudi, or Emirati economies seemed more reliable references than those from the past who'd linked political freedom with free commerce, from Adam Smith to Montesquieu. The market freed consumerist and creative energies, but this time it didn't necessarily liberate societies or political systems. As for Donald Trump, when at the beginning of his term in the name of his emergency economic policy he attacked the democratic institutions that were hindering his momentum— the press, the judicial system, Congress, as well as the traditions of American tolerance—he finalized their divorce, at least rhetorically.

If today more and more economists are criticizing the malfunction of the Chinese system and the authoritarianism of the Gulf countries whose economies are founded on a single natural resource that will soon be depleted, fifteen years ago a number of decision-makers were finally understanding or pretending to discover what was clearly self-evident: that the neoliberal economic machine functioned at full throttle and with the best yield without any need for public opinion, for regular elections, for general consent (whether measured or extorted), or even for guaranteed civil liberties. At the beginning of the third, current phase, the most powerful countries in the world were at war on a number of foreign fronts via the explicit collision of economic interests with geopolitical aims (the ex-vice-president Dick Cheney and his company Halliburton come to mind …). They were also engaged in a social war at home against social movements. All of this was occurring with levels of violence that had been unprecedented in recent decades. This was truly the phase of the real dissociation between representative democracy and a financialized market economy. It marked the final end of a dream or of a lie.

2. The Neoliberal Turn of the 1980s

It all began at the turn of the 1980s with an ideological takeover. Its "pioneers" can be credited with a certain audacity for their time and with an admirable sense of anticipation. Indeed, in the 1970s, the CIA and the Nixon administration's support for the Chilean military that seized power in 1973, the unexpected 1979 election of Margaret Thatcher in the United Kingdom, and the 1980 election of Ronald Reagan in the United States were at once completely unexpected events and pure doctrinal coups. In the beginning, these people were not opportunists. They came to power with ideologues and precise, long-considered arguments that were still minority views but that they hoped would prevail. This translated into the implementation of a certain number of measures: the deregulation and privatization of entire sectors of the economy, the end of industry monopolies, the flexibility of labor, the optimized circulation of capital, and an open hardliner war with the unions and social movements that were attempting to resist (notably the British Yorkshire mines and the French steel and auto industries under "socialist" president François Mitterand). We must remember that in order to be implemented in France, a somewhat special country, this neoliberal wave would require a strange detour facilitated by a president and a number of governments that were labeled as being on the left. For such an ideological change to occur, the French tradition of a redistributive state and its relative indulgence in the face of social rebelliousness required the soothing discourse and reassuring presence of the Left in power. This change went by relatively unnoticed, especially after a few strong symbolic actions had been taken to oppose its repressive logic, such as the abolition of the death penalty, the decriminalization of homosexuality, a fourfold increase in cultural budgets, etc.

Beyond France, we know that the most radical measures taken by German governments to financialize the economy, to modulate the labor market, and to turn industrial labor into precarious labor were implemented more aggressively by Gerhard Schröder's social-democratic (SPD) government in the 1990s than by Helmut Kohl's conservative CDU in the 1980s. In the same way, Bill Clinton zealously finalized the work that Ronald Reagan and George Bush had begun prior to his tenure. In England, the same thing happened with Tony Blair, who added to his predecessor's program the promotion of London as a global financial capital and the neoliberalization of public services, with constant evaluations and cost-effective criteria. This was his famous New Public Management. There was indeed a basic consensus between left and right electoral parties, and the efficiency of the Left consisted in taking less frontal measures, or taking measures that concerned the state structure itself, but which led to the same brutality.

To return to the pivotal moment of the early 1980s, the emblematic event was the clash between the British mining and labor unions and Margaret Thatcher, who revealed herself intransigent to an unprecedented degree. From 1984 to 1987, a bloody repression of strikes in industrial strongholds and massive layoffs in the newspaper industry, occurred with months of struggles in London. The Thatcher government had won the fight with bloodshed. This led to a general demobilization. Those employees who had not been fired felt that being part of a union had become useless. Besides, this phase of political and ideological takeovers was also a time of libertarian and pro–free market convergence during which the countercultural and emancipatory discourse of the previous era was starting to be recycled, this time in the service of business and management. Successively, this would give birth to a more informal business model and to a form of capitalism unrecognizable from its previous incarnations. From then on, it would be "convivial," creative, nomadic, fluid, and its most visible harbingers would be young people, from the start-ups of Silicon Valley to the European nouveaux riches. However, since the convivial firm was continually downsizing, this friendly varnish didn't hold up long. Even if the terms were historically ambivalent—"liberal" meant social permissiveness and in other languages designated an unbridled form of capitalism, whereas "libertarian," especially in the United States, referred to forms of anticonformism on the left as well as on the extreme right—a decisive alliance was formed at the time between the emancipatory themes of the 1960s and the strategic acceleration of the market economy and the privatization of all existence.

But the 1970s and 1980s also witnessed an unprecedented generational convergence between a liberatory groundswell, linked to youth culture and to the struggles of the 1960s, and Western capitalism undergoing accelerated renewal. Offshoring, deindustrialization, conversion to a service economy, precarization of labor, and a new role for culture and the media were at the heart of the economy. Beyond a few emblematic figures of this convergence (such as young, progressive, sneaker-wearing entrepreneurs from Northern California or owners of trendy media outlets), from the 1970s onward the Baby Boomer generation would increasingly associate the forces of capital with the depoliticized legacy of the 1960s revolts. The driving force of this convergence—or rather, of this deliberate misappropriation of the subversive values of the 1960s—was opportunism. And it cannot be attributed to a single generation. It was also the opportunism of architects of an economic system who had diagnosed a structural crisis linked the exhaustion of natural resources, the comparative increase of the price of industrial labor, the emergence of competition from the Third World, and even the entry on the global market of the Eastern Bloc countries after the end of the Cold War. In this context, the convergence between the freedoms of a new generation and the imperatives of profit was fortuitous, and would be praised by all parties involved. Soon after May 1968, advertisements for French supermarkets showed silhouettes of riot police taken from protest posters but who were now bludgeoning … prices! This convergence of interests between a free spirit and a free market included an element of economic necessity—the so-called infrastructural overdetermination, in classical Marxist terms—as well as an element of chance, in the sense of opportunities and fortuitous encounters. Indeed, the new experts in marketing and modern advertising learned to make good use of the fits and starts of current events, including sociopolitical ones.

This rightward turn was thus neither simply a tactical convergence nor the effect of a single generation. In Europe, the previous generation had abandoned its progressive hopes in the trauma of the Second World War. In America, that generation had shifted from a postwar intellectual Left into a conservative movement that former progressives would discretely found in the 1970s. Indeed, that earlier generation carried within it the shift to the right, and in fact willed it. In that sense, the godfathers of American neoconservatism—Irving Kristol, Jeane Kirkpatrick, Norman Podhoretz, Nathan Glazer, Daniel Bell, or Seymour Martin Lipset—did not betray as much as simply readjust their positions. They had always been elitist and moralizing, and simply adapted to the historical mutations of the last third of the twentieth century, many of which they had foreseen before anyone else. The opportunism of young sharks in the 1970s and 1980s and the turnabouts it inspired, has often justified blaming our contemporary disaster on the entire Baby Boomer generation. In reality, it was the opposite. Only a minority defected to the other side, even if this minority was the most visible. The masses of rebellious riffraff tried to manage as best they could without betraying their youthful ideals. If people are less revolutionary in their forties than they were in their twenties, and less inclined to climb onto the barricades or into a paddy wagon, it's not because they have turned their coats but because of a well-known and understandable existential evolution. Yet observers have highlighted the more rare emblematic cases, often blown out of proportion, of those few disheveled revolutionaries who called with great lyrical emphasis for a Marxist-Leninist or libertarian-Maoist revolution when they were eighteen, and who, twenty years later, found themselves at the head of media empires, banks, federal departments, or sitting in Congress, or simply at the heart of the culture industry—in short, all those who slipped, over the course of a few years, from Lenin to Lennon or Stalin to Stallone. In the United States, Jerry Rubin is one such emblematic figure, shifting from the Yippies to the yuppies. So is Abbie Hoffman, who ended up as a Reaganite. In Germany, Joschka Fischer went from anarcho-Maoism to the ministries of the Schröder government. In France, Régis Debray moved from Che Guevara to the cabinets of Mitterand's presidency. These examples are real, but they shouldn't lead us to conclude that there was an overall generational shift. The handful of turncoat progressives who rose to power remain a minority and in no way represent all of their contemporaries. The border is never clearly marked between renunciation and fidelity, just as there is a nuance between betrayal and treachery. If we look at the generational story of the Baby Boomers from the 1960s onward, we see that most of them went from anti-establishment enthusiasm and political activism to forms of disarray or depression, existential crisis, disenchantment, or inner exile. Or, they simply attempted to negotiate or compromise so as not to betray their values too much, and to be neither dominated nor dominant—which is a good start. The balance is always hard to find.

We must also beware of the very concept of generation. It is a naturalizing and biologizing concept that turns a birthdate into the cause and consequence of an individual's behavior. This is a regrettable mistake, if only because we all know seventy-year-olds who are "younger" in mind and attitude than twenty-year-old kids ... And yet the concept of generation remains pertinent if you take into account the collective narcissism of certain age groups and the similar self-promoting or systematically renunciatory behavior that they share. We cannot blame the Baby Boomers for having lived in more favorable conditions than us. They did not choose full employment, the demographic boom, or economic prosperity. If we leave aside the more visible fringe of this generation, those who cynically took power by reversing their prior principles, the rest of this generation, dispersed and condemned to action after the fact, was clearly not in any position to stand against the extreme individualization of forms of life, or against the rise of the neoliberal ideology that they either spearheaded or were victimized by, as the case may be. It is therefore quite difficult to apply an outside judgment to these lived trajectories. When the conditions for the collective management of conflicts and frustrations have disappeared, when unions or parties no longer offer credible recourse, when interpersonal relations no longer exist outside of generalized competition, it becomes difficult to exit from the invisible, supposedly benevolent, and stimulating prison that is mandatory individuality. In other words, "me, me, me" is neither simply the narcissistic chorus sung by Bernard-Henry Lévy, the "New Philosopher" with revealing cleavage, nor the repetitious drone of the former pacifist activist and feminist Hillary Clinton turned belligerent and unsuccessful presidential candidate. It is also the structural effect of a historic turn, a moment when individual self-promotion became an unavoidable precept.

In such evolutions, it is always difficult to distinguish between the resistances or compromises of the individual subject and the great structures of domination. But in order to respect the complexity of historical causality, we must counter the most elaborate analyses of mechanisms of structural domination with all of the resistant ruses and small "arts of doing" in the manner of French philosopher Michel de Certeau.[2] For de Certeau, History, whatever its methods, was an "art of forgetting," an always contextual selection of the phenomena and actors that were worthy of being archived and taking part in a general narrative at the expense of invisible resistances and noninstituted peoples. He was one of the first historians to become interested, as a methodological principle, in all of those who hadn't been inscribed in the dominant narrative. What de Certeau wrote in the 1970s and 1980s makes him a precious author for us today. We need to rediscover his attempt to introduce dissident subjectivity, which is always difficult to totalize (with its micronarratives and "transversal tactics") in the interstices of the diabolical domination that was theorized at the same time by Pierre Bourdieu and Michel Foucault, to whom de Certeau devotes an entire chapter of *The Practice of Everyday Life*. It is a beautiful tactical gesture, a way to reintroduce a dose of optimism, a concern for discrete resistances, minority practices, and alternative epistemologies. In this way, de Certeau goes against the two giants of French critical thought and their macroscopic vision of domination, which is often "fatalizing" and disarming.

Beyond this, it's important to keep in mind that History is not made by individuals, nor even by generations. Sketching a contemporary history through the prism of the concept of generations is not, of course, completely false, but it is very insufficient. Such a history would present the Baby Boomers of 1968 as the "scumbags of History," the only spoiled children of the twentieth century, or affirm that the following generation— the famous "Generation X," as touted by magazines in the early 1980s—was a "lost generation," a generation caught between the triumphant Baby Boomers and the Internet generation. We should be careful not to infer historical causality from a coherent, even monolithic collective subject that does not exist in reality. What is at stake here is as much the violence of men as it is the more invisible, blind force of structural violence.

3. The Ephemeral Euphoria of the 1990s

The second phase of this vast shift to the right is bounded by more tangible events. Two famous falls delimit it, two well-known pivotal dates: the fall of the Berlin wall in 1989, and the fall of the Twin Towers on September 11, 2001. Yet these turning points have so often been invoked that they've become commonplace and we should be wary of them. But it remains nonetheless true that the decade of the 1990s is caught between two collapses. The dismantling of the Soviet Union in 1991, ending our first era, was largely unexpected. When we look at Ronald Reagan's speeches on the "Evil Empire" three years prior, clearly no one fore-saw such a rapid change, a change that would reshuffle the deck on a scale that was hard to understand at the time. The first effect of the col-lapse of the Eastern Bloc on the Western elites was a kind of relief, an ideological and doctrinal dis-inhibition that would suddenly boost audiences for neoliberal ideologues, for historical anticommunists, and for defenders of market democracy from the Atlanticist camp of the Cold War (that is, from Western Europe and North America). In the 1980s, the radical fringe of these ideologues, favorable to global denationalization and to suppressing all forms of social aid, had remained in the minority. From that point on, however, they would be able to force themselves upon the ruling classes. It was as if a single unexpected geopolitical event justified the most doctrinaire of ideologues. One intellectual symptom of the time was the report written for the Rand Corporation, a conservative American think tank, by the historian Francis Fukuyama on the "end of history" and the emergence of the "last man"—that is to say, the effective accomplishment on a global scale of the neoliberal consensus revisited as the Hegelian finality of History.[3]

To the great dismay of the moderate-left parties and of the social democrats who were attached to the principle of a marginal redistribution of wealth by public authority, Margaret Thatcher was elected in 1979 on the idea that there was no alternative to a market economy freed of its state safeguards. But it was only in 1989–91 that the dice were finally cast, and that everyone from the extreme Left to the extreme Right took stock of the end of the so-called alternatives. It was as if

Thatcher's ideological slogan had suddenly become an objective historical fact. The only thing left to do—Thatcherites hoped it would be a no-brainer and a winning bet—was to extend the supposed benefits of market-media democracy and its unquestionable institutions to the Eastern countries that were now finally "free," as well as to all the countries of the Third World.

Disenchantment set in within a few months. In the early 1990s, war and conflict appeared in these supposedly "liberated" countries with access to democratic peace. Yugoslavia was torn apart by civil war and secession, racism and anti-Semitism held sway in Russia, and the student protests in China's Tiananmen Square were brutally suppressed. This is without taking into account the new antagonisms at the heart of the "developing" world, as it was beginning to be called: the Algerian civil war that began in 1992, and the terrible Rwandan genocide of 1994. Neoliberalism—galvanized by the sudden self-destruction of what it had put forth as its only alternative on a global scale, the Soviet dictatorship—believed that it could finally deploy all of its power without fear of opposition and demonstrate the validity of its principles. More precisely, three cardinal principles were at stake. First, was the intrinsically emancipative nature of the market (competition lowers prices and provides universal access to material happiness). Second, was the belief in the concept of self-regulation, which is the metaphysical extension of the natural sympathy linking things and beings postulated by the eighteenth-century physiocrats. And, third, was the the general harmony of the spontaneous balance of supply and demand (Adam Smith's principle of the invisible hand). This lofty, exhilarating program was given a more brutal but very accurate summary in Thatcher's well-known injunction to "Work yourself out of poverty." If you were poor, it was your fault. You were the only one responsible. You therefore had to climb out of it yourself, without expecting anything from the state or from any other institution. From then on, the scrupulous criminalization of any dependent behavior in regard to collective institutions was easy. For the first time, the condemnation of supposed "state handouts" given to the unemployed would become a key element in dominant global discourse. Self-regulation was touted as good news, even a source of ecstasy, which the French thinker Gilles Châtelet derided in his 1998 pamphlet *To Live and Think Like Pigs,* where he wrote of "self-regulation as a festive neoconservatism."[4] As a mathematician, he was interested in the scientific bases of the concept of self-regulation used in disciplines ranging from astrophysics to economics, and demonstrated that the idea according to which phenomena will regulate themselves and harmonize without exterior intervention had, at the time, single-handedly produced a kind of intellectual euphoria on the part of ideologues and of the general public that was similar to a belief in magic.

But projecting the self-regulation of bodies and cells onto human activity poses a problem. Applying the concept to social and political phenomena amounts to biologizing the social and to naturalizing societies, and we know the dangers of that. Irrespective of the concept's scientific value, however, its use—or rather, its abuse—in the 1990s took on a euphoric, at times hysterical tinge at the heart of public space. For it constituted a significant change in regard to Margaret Thatcher's aggressive platform and right-wing social Darwinism in which workers would have to accept unemployment and struggle for survival. From that point on, self-regulation was heralded as something marvelous and exciting. There is certainly a link to be drawn with the appearance of an uninhibited discourse around money, which single-handedly became the supreme sign of self-regulation's miracles. Until that point, easy wealth had been frowned upon. This was the case with the traditional hypocrisy around money that was the norm in Catholic countries. Or, with the Protestant defense of the sobriety of life as a capitalist precept during the industrial revolution, seen in industrialist Andrew Carnegie's philanthropic imperative, or sociologist Thorstein Veblen's criticism of "conspicuous consumption." But henceforth, rapidly accumulated wealth would provoke admiration and unprecedented stardom. The new American heroes of the 1980s—such as real estate magnate Donald Trump, or CNN founder Ted Turner—displayed their wealth as proof of their intrinsically superior value. And in Europe, from the privatization of the public TV channel TF1 (purchased by the Public Works and Engineering tycoon Francis Bouygues in 1987) to the new Russian billionaires whose sparkling yachts and villas supposedly illustrated the virtues of free enterprise, self-regulation supposedly produced magical worlds where apparently everything was luxurious, calm, and voluptuous. Its mendacious principle claimed to be a source of joy, an exhilarating hallucination for uncertain times.

The paradigm underpinning this model was less the all-powerful individual subject dear to the physiocrats and old-style liberals, than cybernetics. This new social science had been invented in American military labs during the Second World War. Its far less humanist project was to create a "man without content" whose imperfect emotions would no longer lead to social warfare, nor impede his access to indefinite progress. The

American army had recruited a number of scientists exiled from Europe, such as John von Neumann, Claude Shannon, and Norbert Wiener. They believed that affect in all of its guises—fear, desire, love, and hate—was the single collective cause of the catastrophe that had been the World War in 1940, or, much later, the economic crisis of 1980. Forms of partially automated regulation, mechanic or electronic, should therefore replace human affects. This was a kind of ideological actualization of the man-machine theory dear to the materialist philosophers of the eighteenth century. Cybernetics could help steer individuals and societies, rationalize social mechanisms, and efficiently regulate affects. This paradigm forcefully reappeared in the period we are looking at, especially since its most effective and revolutionary illustration, the publicly available Internet, emerged simultaneously with its first service providers in the United States in 1991–92. The technophile euphoria of the early digital revolution was an extension of cybernetic ideology. The pioneering thinkers of the Internet touted it as a kind of collective intelligence, an interconnected global brain that would enable the collective self-regulation of social relations, of emotions, and of all dispersed forms of knowledge.

In short, a very real geopolitical event, the fall of the USSR, loosened the tongue and freed the heart, unleashing the enthusiasm of a self-regulated liberal-libertarian society. Whereas hurried journalists described that moment as the "end of ideologies" and a return to the real, the exact opposite occurred: an ideological surge triggered by circumstance, a very sudden reideologization of the world. Yes, there was more ideology in the 1990s' lyrical odes to economic globalization and to generalized self-regulation than during the entire Cold War. One need not be a great dialectician to understand that very few people in the West were convinced Atlanticists, and that even smaller numbers in the East were actual Stalinists. People simulated their beliefs and performed whatever rituals were necessary to survive or just to be left alone. The rise of an extremely worrisome, essentializing Islamophobia in our countries is partly due to the fact that people have forgotten the obvious, as true of 1950s Moscow as it is in Tehran or Cairo today: that a number of people of faith perform the exterior gestures, the required rituals, and the signs that protect against condemnation, in order to give themselves room to maneuver and to make a place for themselves within the dominant order. Such gestures do not necessarily indicate interior adherence, and even less a monolithic community. In a regime that gives people freedom of thought, ideological submission is paradoxically even greater. From the 1990s onwards, at the heart of a world that had been finally "liberated," the idea that self-regulation's transhistorical truth would bypass political divisions, and the notion of the favorable nature of exchange and therefore of an "end of ideologies," was perhaps the most misleading and ideological of the late twentieth century. As Bourdieu reminded us, the end of ideologies was precisely the specific ideology of the time.

Thirty years later, from the new bohemians to the working class, stimulated and compulsory neoliberal individualism is still the most globally shared thing. How was such individualism raised to an absolute? How was such delusional self-regulation and demonization of all social resistance, within us and among us, transformed into natural, unquestionable fact—that is, into the very marker of ideology? The disarming of critique as an individual reaction or a collective creation is always a complex issue. It entails, in part, our immersion in a larger linguistic context, inherent to the language that we speak and to the discursive operators that we use, but also has a more cultural or atmospheric immersion. Ideology is "in the air" as much as in language. And the conveyer belt used to extend this paradoxical ideology was extensively renewed at the time. Let's not forget that the *media* revolution was in full swing. In the twenty-year span from the beginning of our first era to the end of the second, the media landscape shifted from a handful of broadcast TV channels in each country to several thousand channels that could be watched anywhere thanks to cable and satellite services. The average time spent watching TV doubled during this period, and has only started lessening very recently due to competition from the Internet. TV was how all of these ideas were transmitted. But, in any case, the fact remains that neoliberalism in all of its various incarnations corresponds to the exact definition of ideology in Marx and in Althusser: something that presents itself as reality, common sense, or even nature itself to better dissimulate the specific interests at play.[5] By inverting actual social relations, ideology pretends to be a nonideology that would unveil the lie. Whereas, on the contrary, in regard to what is explicitly presented as ideology (religion, for example), we are not compelled to believe because we simply "perform" the belief, and deploy its gestures and exterior decorum.

But let us return to what was essential in this second era—that is, the global and deliberate financialization of the economy that constituted an absolutely decisive stage. This was the moment when stockholders took over capital. What had previously been a familial, patrimonial, or even state capitalism, a system of alliances between institutions and rentiers, became from then on a purely shareholder capitalism, and that much more difficult to challenge in the context of the period. From American investors dabbling in the stock market to the French state denationalizing its large public utilities and listing them on the market, all citizens were encouraged to become small shareholders. Behind the smokescreen of ordinary shareholders, shareholder capitalism, the most nefarious of oligarchies, went so far as to present itself as a form of social progress, a democratic supplement. Throughout the entire "free" world over the course of the 1980s, market news made its TV and radio debut, a huge absurdity for the majority of the population, as it remains today.

Of course, shareholder power belongs to the "big" traders or the "pros," not to the little ones. This shift to shareholder capitalism has turned the world topsy-turvy: in principle, shareholders are supposed to finance firms, but since the 1990s, firms are financing shareholders, with the state itself helping the firms to finance shareholders' returns. This is a complete reversal of the initial logic of the market. And everyone pays the price for it, from workers suddenly declared useless by an audit recommending their firm move offshore, to CEOs who are let go because they did not sufficiently increase profits. This phenomenon is global. Beyond France, reunified Germany, Great Britain, and the United States, the entire Eastern Bloc shifted without any transition from a planned Stalinist economy to an entirely privatized economy, most often in the hands of shady oligarchs and poststate mafias. At the same time, China entered the WTO, which was still something of a surprise. And shareholder fever took hold even in developing countries, which translated to localized crises in the Southeast Asian Tigers and in Central America—soon, the term "tequila effect" would be used to refer to the ripple effect of market instability from one Third World country to another.

These changes occurred in an atmosphere of permanent ideological blackmail that sought to impose trading and microcredit as universal solutions to inequality, or to harness parliamentary democracy by refinancing the state with the stock market, as if this were a self-evident solution. For a few years there wasn't much reaction from the critical Left, since the Left was bearing the brunt of its own critical powerlessness and the terminal shaming of all discourse that remotely referred to social movements, "real" communism, or even, more modestly, the compensatory role of the state. During the crepuscular decade that ended the millennium, the same story circulated everywhere, a dominant discourse with no real retort, or which was only contested in low voices, in the shadows. But this murmur would soon explode.

4. The Marriage of the Market and of Extreme Conservatism

Then came the third era. At the turn of the millennium, a series of phenomena arose that indicated a change. The alter-globalization wave occurred, with its heterogeneous margins and radicalized elements. The wave that would be brutally revealed at the anti-WTO countersummit in Seattle in 1999 but was in fact the result of a series of social awakenings in the mid-1990s, from the Zapatista revolt in Chiapas to the general strikes in France in 1995. This wave would soon crash against the "Clash of Civilizations" doctrine imposed at the expense of all others following the September 11, 2001 attacks. This doctrine's religious, civilizational, and essentializing vision of the West had been proposed in Samuel Huntington's 1997 best-seller, and would be actively, ideologically, and militarily applied by George W. Bush and his administration beginning in the fall of 2001.[6] In broad strokes, a global social movement was rising in reaction to the financialization of the world, but its force was abruptly cancelled and deactivated by the new doctrine. Everything had to bow before a greater, more imminent threat. The "Clash of Civilizations" doctrine was a way to impose torpor, as detailed by Canadian activist Naomi Klein's description of it as a "shock doctrine."[7] The year 2001 can easily be recoded as the year of the great turn. Its date would inaugurate the new millennium and give credence to the great tipping point (or the "software update"). This time, war took over. It was announced everywhere, but its enemy remained fairly undefined, and it became a cover term that justified everything. Because of it, the scattered guerrilla that had emerged to fight the neoliberal conquests of the preceding decade was required to cede immediately to a "war against terror" led by the Americans, with or without their allies—that is to say, by the neoconservative intellectuals of all countries as well as by the United States Army via the occupation of Afghanistan in late 2001 and the invasion of Iraq in 2003. And then, as always, total warmongering was not without its benefits for the world economy, not only in terms of arms sales, but also because its logic allowed for greater social control, more efficient repression, and a more iniquitous appropriation of natural resources. This initiated capitalism's securitarian turn, which had the additional advantage of providing a welcome ideological diversion. During those years, even more so than after the fall of the Berlin Wall, the global anticapitalist movement was presented as criminal and irresponsible. This made sense, since the only true and present danger was named Al-Qaeda, as the new fearmongers kept hammering home. But this phase would be short lived, and last less than ten years.

If we were to write a hypothetical history, we might ask ourselves if this turn would have been as marked without George W. Bush's unexpected, and just barely stolen, victory at the polls in November 2000. What we can say is that nothing, neither an intelligent democratic president nor a majority opposition movement, would have been able to stand up against the ideological alliance between economics, the army, and the state that was cemented in place from 2001 to 2004. No matter what, it would have been deemed necessary to to wash away the indelible blood that had stained the US flag. This was a convenient alliance, but it satisfied long-term structural interests and in the short term constituted a furious, patriotic reaction to what remains the most violent external attack perpetrated on American soil in the country's long history.

During this third phase of the vast attempt to shift the world to the right, the ascending forces whose rise we have just described—the new institutions to generalize competition, the great multinationals, the neoliberal ideologues, and the state oligarchies turned into docile managers of the economic order—would exhibit a certain ideological opportunism. This ruling class, the class of technostructure and of the ideological production of the 1990s, would soon stop viewing the state as an obstacle to the smooth functioning of the market. Rather, it would extol or simply practice its neoliberalization, since the state would suddenly become necessary to shave off deficits, to train precarious workers, to survey everything, and to absorb losses. This was a period during which political and economic leaders converged, often as the same people, as exemplified, for example, by the shuffle of high civil servants between ministries and investment banks. It was also the moment of a new military-political partnership for which American Vice President Dick Cheney was the standard-bearer. Cheney was caught in an unprecedented conflict of interest by contracting his own company, Halliburton, which he had previously directed and in which he was still a shareholder, to become the first private partner of the US Army in the new Iraq war. On a larger scale, the subprime crisis of 2008–9 finalized the collision between the state and big business. Once the real-estate speculation bubble burst and the global economic machine jammed, states had recourse to unprecedented fundraising to save investment banks and insurance and industry giants. Nothing was asked in return, not even the rhetorical promise of a bit more regulation of speculative activity.

The phenomenon was so astounding that it can only be explained by the diehard attitude of economic and state actors. One explanation is certainly the effect of international competition. Any country that did not extend a hand to its banks, or that might have demanded future commitments, ran the risk of having them flee to neighboring countries and thus losing mastery of its own financial economy. Another element was the unprecedented imbrication of political and economic elites, through which they could both swear to a new clairvoyance in regard to the "excesses" of financial capitalism (it is well-known that sobriety is not its cardinal virtue), optimize their own rates of profit, and at the same time impede states, via lobbying or discrete "technical" measures, from slowing down or curbing the circulation of capital. Nonetheless, the 2008–9 bailout was clearly a blank check made out to those primarily responsible for the economic disaster, and this is absolutely astounding. We can even say that if something resembling a global social movement emerged in the last ten years in the wake of this crisis, it was proportionate to the shock that so many felt in the absence of any political reaction to the financial meltdown. The disappearance of political decision-making in the face of the display of the terminal incoherence of financial economy meant that this time we could only count *on ourselves*, and no longer on the state or on elections.

The subprime crisis can be read as the deepest and most direct cause of the social antiestablishment awakenings that would emerge worldwide in the years that followed, from the Spanish *indignados* to the campers who occupied public squares in North America, and from the Arab Spring protestors to the South Korean strikers. The crisis was also the logical cause of the sporadic forms of direct violence that were revealed on the occasion, and the reason behind the new forms of justification of social violence. This time, the link between political representation and the global disaster, or between contemporary suffering and the old "ethics of discussion" that had made modern democracy an arena for discussion, had been broken, and their connection shorn. Since words and programs had lost their promise, this time we could go all out, place our bodies as a barricade against the destruction of the world. The ease with which elected officials and corporate leaders continued to act post-2008 as if nothing had happened, when they did not simply remove the last remaining protections against speculative folly, led a number of people to a simple and radical conclusion about the historical obsolescence of discussion, negotiation, and elections. In Occupy Wall Street tents, in South American squares, and in Nuit Debout France, it was obvious that any discussion with those people was useless since they completely disregarded their pious promises and their principles of moderation at the exact moment when they pushed them to the forefront, as if to make amends. This was drastically different from the end of the 1990s, when the social movement awoke (following the neoliberal turn of the 1980s) with the rise of the extreme Left in a few countries through local and national elections. This time, the debate was no longer between antiestablishment anarchists who didn't vote and opportunistic leftists ready to risk representation, because neither seemed to believe in elections any longer. They would simply do without.

We can even say that the one-upmanship by state-financial elites of the very mechanisms that caused the bankruptcy was quite literally "fundamentalism." At the very moment when its efficiency had been jeopardized, and when its intrinsic vices had been universally revealed, the system in place hysterically intensified its principles, and imposed unprecedented levels of social violence with its headlong rush. In a sense, the operative mechanism of this kind of blindness, for which violence is the only possible outlet, is not dissimilar to jihadist indoctrination and suicide attacks. Of course, this is simply a metaphor, but it conveys how both sides abandoned logic altogether. An anonymous text published after the November 13, 2015 attacks in Paris explained that the attacks were a vain, pathetic face-to-face between two fundamentalisms, economics and religion, to which

the mysterious authors suggested one should substitute a "communism of the sensible."[8] In any case,
these three successive eras—the takeover of the
1980s, the doctrinal euphoria of the 1990s, and the
ideological opportunism and repressive one-
upmanship of the 2000s—structured the long turn
to the right of the last half century.

There were of course continuities on the part of
managerial, individualizing, and neo-identitarian
forces, but we must admit that this right-wing
neoliberalism is protean, and that it does not
constitute a coherent ideological entity. It does,
however, possess an initial doctrinal corpus. This
was centered around the Lippmann symposium held
in Paris in 1938, attended by economists such as
Friedrich Hayek, and texts from the Mont Pelerin
Society assembled in Switzerland in 1947, authored
by Hayek as well as Milton Friedman, Karl Popper,
etc. It is interesting to reread Hayek to measure this
evolution. He had proposed a radical antistatism
less in the name of economics than because of a
particular historical sensibility to the question of
totalitarianism, and a kind of social and existential
anarchism that was not uninteresting. But what
neoliberalism subsequently became bears no relation
to this primary impetus, and was dictated instead
by circumstances and successive crises. We can refer
to it as "ideological opportunism," in the sense that
it constructed a complex architecture with elements

added or removed according to historical contexts and what opposition it encountered.

It remains that the third phase, which we are still in, represented an unprecedented and unpredictable alliance between the neoliberals and the neoconservatives, between the defenders of a total, unfettered market and the champions of moral, patriotic, and "civilizational" values that used to be classified as part of the extreme Right. The same collusion of interests between the hubris of optimal profit and the model of a repressive security state, a circumstantial but decisive alliance, is what in the end characterizes the right-wing turn. For, theoretically, this alliance is unnatural. The corpus of neoliberal doctrine is very nonconformist, and is not backward looking. Through progressive and purely economic logic, it loathes historical legacy and safe choices. All of this has more to do with the libertarian anarchism inherited from the 1960s and 1970s than with traditional conservatism. And yet, on the other side is the system of traditional, ethnocentric, Christian, and even imperialist or explicitly xenophobic values. It is now shamelessly defended by Trump or Putin (and, in other countries, by so many other elected leaders and opinion makers), when it had long been the prerogative of a minority fringe of the ruling class. Circumstances specific to the 2000s led to the alliance of these two movements. The result was a broad-spectrum rhetorical and ideological moloch that accelerated the decline of the Left. Indeed, in terms of publics and themes, the moloch in question was able to cover a vast domain—ranging from scientific and technological audacity to the creation of social and solidary businesses, and to the new green capitalism by way of Christian fundamentalism, populist editorializing, and fanatic cultural Western-centrism. The size of the occupied area almost mechanically explains the electoral victories of right-wing parties so frequent in the last thirty to forty years, as the left-wing journalist Thomas Franck showed in his 2004 book, *What's the Matter with Kansas?*[9] In this book, Franck attempted to understand what had led the poorest American electors, who stood for social redistribution rather than for the financialization of the economy, to vote Republican, against their immediate economic interests. It came down to "issues," as the themes of an electoral campaign are called, and in particular spontaneous issues around mores: social and moral questions from abortion to the death penalty, from family values to gun laws, questions that traditional American conservatives are obsessed with. For we must not forget that neoliberal punks and libertarians are of course a minority in this new, expanded right-wing grouping. What is new is the convergence of discourses and strategies between these two distinct families. In passing, we should also note that one of the reasons for the rhetorical turn against free trade on the part of the traditional extreme-right parties, from the Tea Party to the National Front, was not only a strategy to recuperate the working-class electorate abandoned by the Left, but also a fiendishly effective tactic to seduce the ruling classes—by playing on their ideological frustration, and on their concern about values faced with the wave of unbridled anti-statist neoliberalism and its insolent relativism.

Although not entirely unnatural, this alliance remains circumstantial, boosted by the profound evolution of capitalism and the recent transformations of the relationship (and equilibrium) between the North and the South. Indeed, the global distribution of wealth is becoming more complicated, since there is a growing macroeconomic inequality between North and South, on the one hand, whereas, on the other, a number of developing countries are becoming leading economic powers, with very powerful ruling classes and sometimes more millionaires than in countries with old wealth. Moreover, income disparities are also exponentially growing in the West, where the economy of financial profit and of conspicuous consumption has ballooned out of control, hence the resurgence of national and identity-based values to reassure the ruling classes as well as the disadvantaged victims of this collision course. And both of these groups refer this unstable and troubling world back to more familiar cultural and religious distinctions: the others might also be capitalists, certainly, but Westerners are also Christian, and heirs to great cultural traditions, and this is where their power and superiority supposedly lie.

But we are speaking here of the ruling classes, and of only part of them. For the rest of public opinion, neoliberal globalization has not *directly* provoked a return to identitarian and national values, but has worked obliquely to make people more sensitive to discourse around identitarian responses and compensatory pride. Once again the issue of the nation is *molding* discourse, but in a new way. Rather than ascribing this kind of compensation to the slippery notion of identitarian or "cultural insecurity," it is more productive to look at *discursive formations* (as Michel Foucault would say) and their recent historical genealogy, and to be attentive to mutations in the nature and the exercise of power. The historical rhythm with which modern national identities were established was relatively slow, in a process that began at the end of the eighteenth century and in reality lasted nearly two centuries. Whereas, following the Second World War and national disenchantment, and with the molting of capitalism under the auspices of a Cold War that shifted the problem, the practical and ideological dissolution of national identities occurred much faster. It happened in one or two decades, with the individualization and the globalization of ordinary life, and the appearance of new transnational entities such as the European Union and the Pacific Zone. The nation used to be everything. In some sense it seems to have disappeared into thin air in twenty years. The speed with which these changes occurred opened an avenue to reactionary ideologues theorizing a return to identitarian values. Yet this return is not the direct and mechanical effect of economic globalization itself: that kind of reductive reasoning is dangerous in the sense that it comes down to legitimizing such identitarian closure. We must take into account psycho-existential and institutional factors, and each country's historical specificities. In France, for example, repressed colonial phantoms are returning to haunt a pluralist nation that is braced against its own principles, with a "color-blind" conception of the state that refuses to recognize the existence of specific identities and communities and their historical traumas, and an assimilationist dogma that is still quite tenacious. This explains the strong right-wing temptation on the part of certain electors, as well as the malaise of postcolonial immigrants in France.

Beyond this, the old elegies to rootedness have been brandished everywhere through the cult of heritage and the obsession of memory. Of course, the Right does not possess a monopoly on the cult of official history. But it is striking to note that, since the time it began to distance itself from its redistributive and social functions at the turn of the 1980s, the state itself has often orchestrated this strategy of reenchanting the nation and its heritage with full-scale memorial commemorations. As historian Enzo Traverso would say, celebrating the victims and the heroes of the nation has become a kind of "state religion."[10] In the midst of crisis, the idea is to divert and to reassemble. But this is of course the effect of a foreclosure, and of the incapacity to represent the future at a moment when uncertainty has become time's only organizing principle in a capitalist world extoling interdependence and complexity. In the face of all this, returning to a fetishized past made of gadgets and to a campy, familiar history—whether it celebrates John Hancock or Charles de Gaulle—is supposed to reassure everyone. Reacting to temporal chaos by resuscitating the past can also occur more spontaneously through community or local initiatives. The nation-state often seems a more abstract reality than provinces or cities, which favor more spontaneous events around local memory, from village museums to yellowed family albums, or now with Internet social networks such as Classmates.com. But at base, the problem lies in our unprecedented inability to think the future, an inability that is due to the acceleration of social time, to a future that seems completely obstructed, and to an exacerbated "presentism," a concept coined by historian François Hartog to designate the extension, ad infinitum, of an automatic present that is emptied of its contents and sheared from its roots and possibilities.[11] But let's be careful not to generalize. This sudden need to take refuge in a collective, personalized, and collectively modified past is more generalized in the West. In other parts of the world the past can constitute the very life of the household, as is the case in societies where people exist *with* the dead, for example, with altars honoring lost family members often placed in the middle of living rooms as an integral part of culture.

Without falling prey to culturalist clichés feeding into tourist folklore, beyond Western countries and their dogma of modernity as rupture, tradition often bears more weight and is more apt to support individual and collective forms of life. Intact traditions often coexist more harmoniously with the modern violence of rupture in societies where individual subjectivity can better confront neoliberal anomie and instability because subjectivity is more collectively framed. This is the case, in differing ways, in Japan, in China, and in Southeast Asia. In the Euro-American world, psychic fragility is often the consequence of a crumbling tradition that is loudly delegitimized. After all, we are children of modernity, a modernity that laid out the insolent project of overtaking and destroying tradition in the nineteenth century. This tradition, pushed out the door, is now coming back through the window, like so many other things. Modernity was a project that meant to impose, at best, a progressive dogma and a continuous program to improve living conditions. In its hysterical version, it imposed permanent, potentially apocalyptic change, and a tearing away from ancient foundations that was all the more violent given that it was compulsory and unanimously praised. This was for a long time the teleological horizon of modernity, its eschatology that implied the erasure of the ordinary past and the pulverization of tradition in order to make progress possible. The great narrative of modernity entered into crisis a long time ago, and we are even supposed to have entered "postmodernity." Without revisiting the haziness surrounding the term—or the powerlessness that it highlights around the capacity to think our historical moment—one of the aspects of postmodernity is certainly this return to a reassuring past, and to a heritage that can be made subjective, a slightly embarrassed reconnection with Tradition that hesitates between irony and need.

2

ORDER, TECHNICS, LIFE

The world shift to the right over the last half century also corresponds to the timeframe of a very large-scale technical, cultural, and even anthropological mutation. It is impossible to bypass the relation between the two. Indeed, at the heart of our historical sequence is also a major technological revolution and its considerable economic consequences, a revolution set in motion in the 1990s with the dual emergence of the Internet for the general public and of cell-phones with their massive market. We are still in the midst of it, and it is difficult to evaluate the scale of this revolution today, even if superlatives abound: it is a mutation equivalent to the appearance of the popular press at the end of the nineteenth century, or to the emergence of the printing press in the sixteenth century, or even to the invention of writing in the Sumerian world. More concretely, the first immediate effect of this emergence was a kind of economic suction, with increased productivity and newly born sectors with very large growth potentials, which in the early days translated into intense market excitement. This "new economy" disrupted all the production processes of industrial and financial capitalism—their rhythms, their modalities, their spirit—and led to the rapid increase of profit rates in the sectors concerned. Capitalism—which we know had been in crisis since the 1970s due to the deindustrialization of developed countries, the foreseeable exhaustion of natural resources, and the financial instability created by neoliberalism—was suddenly stimulated. Here, it found a historical opportunity to bounce back, and entered a new phase.

1. Market Uses of the Digital Revolution

We could draw a history of this technological revolution in three parts, approximately following the three-decade schema we've previously evoked. First, in the 1980s, cell phones and the Internet were not yet on the market, but industrial operators and institutional investors were working on future tools—that already existed technically— and made use of advertising pressure and a kind of anticipated promotion orchestrated by state power to disseminate them, from the first US federal programs on information superhighways to the case of the Minitel in France. At the time, this latter device, which was quickly seen as obsolete due to its missed convergence with the computer, nonetheless provoked a vast debate on the digitalization of society and created anticipation for mutations that would occur the following decade. In 1987, two-thirds of French households possessed a Minitel. France was thus fifteen years ahead of the US, given that the rate of US households with Internet access would only reach two-thirds of the entire population by the year 2000. The future Silicon Valley powers came to the fore during the 1980s, especially in terms of equipment suppliers and software producers (Apple, IBM, Microsoft, etc.). In this phase, although new technologies were not yet radically changing people's lives, nor really disrupting economic activity, a new ideology was settling into place that made digital tools and their connection to the Web a normative obligation, and in the early days provoked a wave of panic among the average consumer, in particular among older generations who felt overwhelmed.

The second phase, during the 1990s, corresponds to the spectacular rise of mobile telephony and of the public Internet. Besides the economic boom it led to, however, this was also a phase of pioneering usage and early daring. At the risk of seeming excessively romantic, I think we can label this moment a "temporary autonomous zone," to use the famous expression by the American writer Hakim Bey.[1] This was a time in which digital production (still quite limited in terms of access) enjoyed fairly extensive political and cultural autonomy, and even a time of sedition, insolence, and originality that would be short-lived. We should specify that the rates of Internet connection were still low, and that this was the time of Web 1.0. The Web was only used to send emails, as a means to get informed via readable data, or to exchange still images at best, with all of this occurring at a speed that remained frustrating.

The third phase was inaugurated by the passage to Web 2.0 at the turn of the millennium. This meant an increase in bandwidth and in connection speed that enabled the exchange and downloading of animated images and sound files. In a few short years it led to the creation of the great *majors* of the infrastructural organization of the Internet such as Google, and to the appearance of new browsers and social-network pioneers such as MSN and, in 2002, Facebook. In this last phase, we witnessed the colonization by traditional market capitalism of that terra incognita that had been the Internet for the previous decade, with the digitization of social and private life, the optimization of profit rates, and the concentration and financialization of the digital economy (which was henceforth no longer referred to as "new"). The global implosion of the speculative bubble around this new economy in 2000 marked a major shift. It imposed a return to reality—that is, to the classical imperatives of profit and of predictable profitability. Economic reason came to call back to order a virtual economy that had been untethered from dominant logic for a few years in an anarcho-libertarian parenthesis, or in a folly based on outlandish ideas: on information that didn't yet exist, or even on hot air or structurally unprofitable projects, like those over-the-top start-ups for which it was not unlikely to raise ten million dollars over drinks during informal weekly meetings between investors and entrepreneurs. In a few words, you could suggest producing a device for long-distance multisensory stimulation with a combination of electrodes, or simply an entertainment website for pets, and win the jackpot. With the first bankruptcies and capitalist offensives following the year 2000, all this returned to normal, or at least to the ordinary and more normative economic disorder.

However, as shown by the contemporary utopia around the sharing economy, such a mutation can foster extraeconomic exchanges (cooperation and barter) as well as multinational conquest strategies, just as it can allow for the circumvention of censorship or selection via educational credentials, or spellbind Internet users with limitless gaming or the online pornography supermarket. Each time, it depends on the usages of the technical tools in question, and on those who control or program them. Usage also lets us judge the scope of the mutation in question. Some have labeled this mutation a "revolution," in the sense that it induces, on the cognitive level, a modification of perception, of knowledge, and of modes of reading the world. Although they do not yet qualify this new age, they envision it as a departure from the five to ten centuries during which the printed book was at the heart of the system of power-knowledge, with its exhaustive, linear, and vertical approach to knowledge. With the appearance of the Internet, we are, it's true, moving toward a modular, lateral, horizontal, and nonexhaustive approach to knowledge: each hyperlink refers permanently and in random ways to other information without it being possible to read everything or for an order of reading to impose itself on all others.

Since the 1990s, several authors have attempted to theorize this revolution at the risk of blending accurate intuition with lyrical fantasies or magical thought. This was the moment when the concept of collective intelligence began to circulate as a debatable hypothesis. Likewise, the first essays cowritten by Antonio Negri and his American colleague Michael Hardt proposed the idea that this lateral connection of everyone with everyone else, read through Marx's concept of the *general intellect*, would necessarily lead to a revolutionary attitude of resistance and invention: in sum, keyboards in the service of the revolution.[2] All this is highly debatable. What is certain, on the other hand, is that the Internet lateralizes, and thus to a certain extent automatically levels hierarchies in social relations, making previous instances of legitimization in part obsolete, especially in the cultural and scientific fields, while facilitating an immediate and random connectivity that disrupts all fields of knowledge and their organization.

In addition, the old dichotomy that organized the production of dominant knowledge and language, separating producers from consumers, authors from readers, has practically become outdated. The phenomenon quickly rose to prominence in the cultural industry. Until then, major labels had decided what records would sell according to industrial strategies and market studies, but musical buzz and self-releasing suddenly cut back on this power. The major publishers, armed with their symbolic capital, had imposed norms and authors; online recommendation modalities destabilized them. And the large film studios that had been courted by all the screenwriters on the planet saw their role of selection and legitimization questioned over the course of a few years, and their economic power largely eroded. This time, competition came out of nowhere, and professionals were powerless to address it. They could not do anything faced with high-school novels written via text messages on smartphones in Japan, or with viral videos on YouTube whose humor or banality instantaneously triggered more views than the big-screen block-busters yielded at the box office. That said, in the political field as in the cultural industry, the old hierarchical structure, when shaken, always resists, and has not as yet been replaced by any other power structure. And the news industry, an entire economic and cultural bisecular model founded on the collection, the publication, and the sale (or exchange for advertisement) of non-specialized information, bore the brunt of the digital revolution. After the devastating effects of infotainment and free newspapers, this added blow was fatal for the viability and even the overall legitimacy of the news media. Today, everything must be reinvented, both in terms of economic models and of communication strategies. Some of the familiar protagonists of the end of the twentieth century, the major newspapers and the most influential radio and TV shows, suddenly found themselves with an expiration date, with-out it being clear what would replace them, or play an equivalent role for the masses or for investors on the lookout. The mutation was more or less brutal according to the sector it affected.

Book and film editors, for example, the disappearance of which had been prognosticated since the early days of the Internet, have better resisted until now thanks to an evolution of their modes of financing (for film) and to niche effects (for books). But their purview has been reduced, and over time their lack of profitability is inevitable. Royalty revenues are shrinking, when they are not in danger of disappearing completely, and the figure of the artist-creator also runs the risk of vanishing in favor of the freelance DIY enthusiast. That change is also important. Replacing the myth of the exceptional genius typical of the great Western artistic tradition, the inventor of today's popular forms is more often than not an ordinary person (as in the case of YouTube stars), or a player, a combiner, a DIYer who is a crazy graphic designer or a covert DJ. Although saying this has become quite commonplace, it's not a mere coincidence that these are the emblematic figures of our postmodern culture, with their palette of technical tools, their chaos of found objects, their recourse to collage and to parody, their refusal to occupy the center stage, and their shadow of mystery and anonymity—a far cry from the classical geniuses and the modern stars with their limelight.

The star system is not on the verge of disappearing in either music or film. However, we can see a mutation in the status of works, and in the modalities of their production. Perhaps it is the classical notion of "cultural *creation*" that is becoming in part obsolete. From music to literature to visual arts, the question is mainly how to recombine the found objects of the vast cultural rubbish heap of modernity in novel ways, how to move through the runoff of modern culture along subjective itineraries to lead it elsewhere or to recompose it differently. This is the case, at least, for today's global youth, whose figureheads are DIY videographers with unpredictable chances of success, DJs or other sound tinkerers, and community activists or activist geeks who are much more in the shadows than the stars of yesteryear—not everyone has the notoriety or the history of Julian Assange, the founder of WikiLeaks. From the point of view of models of innovation and of up-and-coming public personas, motors of identification are no longer geniuses, with their exceptional character (and the hierarchy of disciples and admirers they provoke), but rather the common connected citizen who knows how to turn the ordinary into a source of creation and eventual fame. This transition is less an ethical change than a mechanical consequence, in this case a consequence of the forms of unprecedented interactivity enabled by the new technologies. You can do anything with them and everyone using them is present in the same way at the same time; this is more democratic than the academy, which was inaccessible for the amateur painter, or the Oscars, which remain out of reach for someone who dabbles in video. But the lottery of random celebrity, market services, and reusable (and sellable) data generated online, alongside the network surveillance by a few superpowerful conglomerates that were the first to capitalize the global market in the century, imply that the cultural and cognitive revolution in question is necessarily connected to the reinforcement and the renewal of market logics.

Beyond all of this, our very relation to time has been affected by the upsurge of the Internet, and this has happened on all levels: through the erasure of distance in space and time, through the microsegmentation of attention span, through the constant updating of all information, through the storage and therefore the infinite availability of images and texts, and through an unprecedented layering of different temporalities that remain nonetheless present to one another. There is the time of the breaking news story, the time of the message that interrupts my flow; there is the time period or zone that is far away but in which I can take refuge, right now, plus the way biological duration and socioeconomic time follow their course offscreen … This whole new polychronic reality upsets the clear succession of the past, the present, and the future. But today, this time—or *these* times—of online life are also a source of problems for the capitalist elite and for the global economic macrostructure, because they tear us one after the other from the TV screen, from poorly paid office duties, or from the ordinary family life to which they'd worked decades to harness us. It's like a fold of time where capital and its slogans have a harder time reaching us. This is today's great unknown: Will this interstice extend itself indefinitely, and threaten the system in place, or will the system colonize and reclaim it? In fact, what has been developed since the beginning of the millennium and the passage to Web 2.0 under the auspices of a sharing economy, cooperation, and even random free stuff has brutally reduced revenues in a number of sectors from the press to the music industry by modifying users' behavior and reducing their availability to be monopolized by capital. In the background lie the cognitive and existential stakes of *attention*, the most precious raw material of the global economy.[3] For now, there is a drastic reduction of our average attention span, which used to be linked to the model of the book or of the work meeting and which is now reduced to a handful of minutes, or even seconds. In the long run, the modes of producing attention will need to be reinvented, or at least redesigned.

The problem here is not the occupation of time, which has *always* been occupied—to distance us from ourselves and from others—but rather the duration of cognitive attention and the excessive demands made upon it. Of course, we are not saying "things were better in the past," but underscoring that a modification of forms of attention is underway. The incessant influx of emails or text messages, or the synching of mailboxes and social networks several times a minute, cannot help but influence our attention by calling upon it well beyond our will and our capacities. But most importantly, attention has become the central object of the capitalist economy. It is what this economy is seeking to capture, much more so than natural resources, labor forces, or monetary capital. The phenomenon already existed with TV, as the CEO of a TV channel reminded us when he spoke of selling "available brain time" to advertising agencies. But it has grown in importance. From the print news media (whose golden age in terms of distribution occurred at the turn of the twentieth century), to radio, to TV (whose pinnacle of power was in the 1980s), and up to the digital revolution today, attention has become the principal resource that economic and political powers seek to capture. The filtering of personal data on websites and social networks has replaced advertising. And the celebrity of the star has ceded to the random viral dissemination of anonymous videos. Attention gets collected, although still in an arbitrary way and via very expensive algorithms; it's no longer "won."

However, in this battle for attention, the multinational Web corporations, the multinational pushers of planned obsolescence, and even the conspiracy-theory ideologues and/or conservatives are in ambush, ready to hit the jackpot and to occupy most of the terrain—the terrain of available attention that has shifted to the right. In the face of their powerful capture devices, hackers of all countries would need to unite against Google, Facebook, Rush Limbaugh, or Bill Mitchell. But *in itself*, the media machine is neither on the left nor on the right. We need to remain "antisubstantialist" in terms of technology. Technology does not exist as such—as a substance separate from the social field, from the course of history, and from power relations. Only *usages* exist that decide its shape and destiny. Since we cannot separate machines from their usages, we should be wary of the in-principle, cynical, and self-interested technophilia of many of the Internet pioneers who, in working for the MIT Media Lab or for the large think tanks, were suggestion boxes for American capitalism. We should be just as skeptical of the most caricatural technophobes, from conservatives to working-class advocates, who see technology as the source of all evil and consider it to be leading to an imminent apocalypse. From this point of view, we would be better served to follow a Deleuzo-Guattarian line, one that would be even more Guattarian than Deleuzian if we remember that Felix Guattari, who died in 1992, had witnessed the birth of the Minitel and had considered with great enthusiasm a whole subversive and countercultural potential of telematics networks. The same holds for TV. In the culturally effervescent New York of the early 1990s, nothing was more surprising than community public-access TV providing local breaks from mainstream TV, neighborhood by neighborhood, in a city where local TV networks were being invented by and for the people who lived there … These programs were often disappointing because of their low production values, but they had the advantage of proving that you could do something other than NBC or even HBO with this media. These public-access networks were an absolutely absolutely necessary media that was demonized by elitist intellectuals at the time. In sum, if the Internet has become a multiheaded monster, and TV a force that standardizes the world in the image of Fox News or ESPN, this is due to their powerful financiers much more than to the media themselves. Counterusages are always possible.

In 2003–4, when mainstream American media outlets covered up the official lies of the Bush administration on the presence of weapons of mass destruction in Iraq, alternative, civic, non-professional, and democratic news websites were quickly set up and allowed for a certain popular reclaiming of information in regard to the discredited dominant media. Even earlier, we can recall the underground or partly underground free radio stations in the early 1980s in Europe, ranging from prison broadcasting to the anarchist or separatist enclaves of the FM dial. Everything is a question of usages, and it makes no sense, therefore, to condemn or glorify Technology as such. But to return to the essential question, the digital revolution was clearly a decisive tool in the takeover of our lives and of global history by a new type of neoliberal securitarian system at the turn of the millennium. History could have taken another route entirely.

Once again, this was a system in which Californian anarcho-libertarians rubbed shoulders with the East Coast moneyed bourgeoisie. Its celebrated pioneers—Bill Gates, Mark Zuckerberg, Steve Jobs, or Jeff Bezos—were never Marxist-Leninist guerilla fighters or even the founders of hippy communities, but just people starting businesses with their buddies in a new area under very informal frameworks. In fact, with the (double) generation of entrepreneurs, this was less a turn than a historical convergence. And less a question of personal renunciation than an internal mutation toward advanced capitalism's modes of production in the early stages of its Californian avant-garde, and, by way of this, an ideological modification of capitalist doctrine. The stakes concerned the passage from a patrimonial, familial, Western, socially inert, monopoly capitalism (whose model is Christian and bourgeois), to a sui generis anarcho-libertarian type of capitalism that advocates for the laterality and horizontality of social relations and claims pleasure and contingency as organizing principles. The players of this shift operated in part for cynical reasons, by diverting the free spirit of the 1960s and their own youth culture, but with the sincere goal of deposing the existing monopolies—to change the world, of course, but also to take their place. There is a partially counter-intuitive continuity between the countercultural spirit blowing through California in the 1960s and 1970s and the constitution of these new spaces for dematerialized production and reflection that would contribute to privatizing our lives and to infinitely extending market logics. A continuity, in other words, between the hippy commune and the famous picture of the original Microsoft team in plaid shirts—or, more metaphorically, between Woodstock and Uber, or from radical feminism to popular shareholding. This is not to say that the rot had already set in, but simply that we must not lose sight of an underground continuity. This remains, however, a relative continuity, for there was a qualitative leap in the early 1970s, at the beginning of the period we are interested in, which did not occur in these people's individual trajectories (that's why they never disavowed their point of view) but which was an internal shift in the countercultural movement from the collective to the individual or to the intersubjective, and from an emphasis on politics to a focus on culture. That existential turn and the depoliticization of driving antiestablishment forces put an end to the previous historical cycle, that moment of youthful rebellions and of postwar progressive battles, and inaugurated the great shift to the right.

Take the case of Students for a Democratic Society (SDS), the large leftist American union at the heart of the protests of the 1960s. They were the ones responsible for launching campus sit-ins against the Vietnam War, and were able to create one of the only white alliances with the African American civil-rights movement via the use of anticapitalist rhetoric that resembled the language used by European leftists and communists. This political option lost its strength in the early 1970s because most of the SDS's young members became more interested in the legalization of drugs, in the distribution of new music, or in alternative secessionist forms of life, than in frontal political opposition to the powers that be, something they felt had become useless. This problem, encountered late in the game by the radical Left of the 1960s, has surfaced *mutatis mutandis* again today. What options are left if you don't want to seize power? Today, young secessionists tell us that we need to change forms of life, to decolonize minds, and to liberate gestures and modes of production—which can also occur through the digital revolution. And in 1960s America, it is important to remember that the countercultural movement was in large part based in the libertarian tradition—that is to say, in a system of thought opposed to all forms of state control or central administration. This would facilitate the dissociation between the cultural or existential (even anthropological) project and the strictly political project that many ex-rebels of the 1960s would forgo—since they were less interested than their European counterparts in its later translations into state or electoral forms.

In this way, we can better understand the continuity of the anarcho-libertarian spirit of the 1960s with the young entrepreneurs of Silicon Valley. The "existential" rebels of the early 1970s, just like the denim-clad geeks of early microcomputing, would accompany and in large part shape this internal mutation of capitalism—which in a few years would become mostly a protean informational apparatus whose major resource is cognitive, conceptual, and symbolic, and no longer simply the appropriation of natural resources and of the financial ownership of the means of production. A great number of these new businesses are now public, and their principal shareholders are also their owners. But let's not forget that after the burst of the speculative bubbles, the financial economy gained the upper hand once again and put an end to the anarcho-libertarian era, an era that had already been endangered by the conservative counterrevolutions of the 1980s and the financialization of the economy in the 1990s.

That said, there are, fortunately, many examples of an emancipatory political use of the Internet. But these mostly took place within its cultural margins, or against directly coercive political regimes. They also occurred in the early years of the prehistory of the Internet that some describe as a "temporary autonomous zone"—that is, on the subversive or antifascist platforms of the 1990s, or during the Arab Spring protests of 2011–12. But for the most part, the major technological mutation that thrust all of us into a haze and lined the pockets of futurologists and prophets of the "posthuman" unquestionably contributed to political demobilization, to the disintegration of the large collectives, and to the individualization of all behavior. And of course social movements such as those of the Arab Spring or grassroots initiatives in the West were not born on Snapchat or Facebook. They simply used them before disseminating their movements offline. It is important to distinguish between causes and means, and to remind ourselves that the network only played the role of an instrument—even if it was an indispensable one, certainly, since it is essential to be able to communicate behind the backs of the police in a dictatorship. Although they still remain isolated from one another, these temporary usages are essential, and range from the viral ecological petition to the more rare popular uprising synchronized online. But for all that, we cannot ignore that the Internet, over the course of the two or three decades since it established itself, has mostly contributed to atomizing and "impotentizing" society, to use another word coined by Felix Guattari.

But most importantly, after twenty-five years of the digital revolution, the presence of the large capitalist corporations in our lives has grown more intimate than ever. Add to this the unprecedented development of biotechnologies, and the other great question arises of the impact of the biopolitical, to use Michel Foucault's term—that is, the impact of new digital or biological technologies on our bodies, our minds, and our lives. The biopolitical question—that is, the political (and economic) control of life—is indeed at the heart of this historic shift. It would be a mistake to believe that this global, neoliberal, and right-wing turn consecrated the triumph of laissez-faire ideology and the end of the interference of the state and public authority in our lives, reverting society to a kind of feudal state where everyone is left to their own devices and to the rule of the market. There is indeed a feudal dimension in this turn, in light of the new violence of social relations, but nothing is more false than this idea of laissez-faire ideology. Let us return to Foucault's major intuition in his 1979 seminar at the Collège de France, *The Birth of Biopolitics*.[4] I call it an "intuition" because this seminar opened up just as many problems as it clarified. His idea was as follows. Neoliberalism cannot be defined via the negative as a withdrawal of the state, as the laissez-faire operations of market forces, or as a subtractive faith in the simple capacity of individual entrepreneurial initiative. It must also be defined in a positive or substantive way, as the logic of the normalization of human life on all sides, the extension to all aspects of existence of a politico-economic regime that had previously only impacted certain areas of our life. From cellular life to the lives of consumers or local communities, there is in fact no dimension of life that can escape the supposedly benevolent grasp of the market, and of its state managers and its experts with their new insurance mindset. The global Right has in a sense carried out its "vitalist" turn around the biopolitical, around its marketing of the intimate and its instruments of systematic control. If social vitalism was a left-wing idea and an anarchist or socialist practice at the end of the nineteenth century, a century later it has become the great conquering strategy of neoliberals and neoconservatives—not only for the conquest of power, but for the conquest of all of our lives.

2. The Stimulation of Bodies, the Management of Life

Rather than make a list of the sociopolitical actors, we can slice up the human body and see in cross-section how each region has been colonized and occupied by a mixture of public institutions, media operators, normalizing forces, and economic interests—which stimulate it and want the best for it. At the top, the head: from now on, the psyche is managed by a medical straightjacket and by a whole range of specialized services from Lacanian psychoanalysis to behavioral therapies, via media that flatter our narcissisms and our superegos, and by the crucial double horizon of neuroscience and artificial intelligence. From cosmetics to meditation, from social-network opinion polls to hip talk-shows, our heads are caught in a collection of norms and social skills that are more numerous and oppressive than their ostensible benevolence lets on. Next, we can move down the body and consider, for example, the lungs. Between the mid-1990s and the end of the 2000s, most developed countries passed legislation prohibiting smoking in public places. The rationale behind these bans revealed the triumph of a conception of life and of public space based on insurance, and on the concept of the risk society, which is the basis of the principle of precaution.[5] Basically, rather than go after the macropower of the tobacco industry, individual behavior was criminalized under the pretext of prevention, and blamed for the increase in social welfare deficits and even for the death of peers through second-hand smoke.

Modern biopolitics was invented during the second half of the nineteenth century, with practices ranging from medical hygiene to the first crackdowns against alcohol, and from the first birthrate politics (either pronatalist or Malthusian) to the rants of proponents of raciology on the "born criminal" (inspired by Italian anthropologist Cesare Lombroso's ideas around racial hierarchies and skull shape). But a century later, the double digital and pharmaceutical turn of the end of the twentieth century gave it a major boost. For this, we must take into account the passage, analyzed by Michel Foucault, from the disciplinary societies of early modernity to our contemporary societies of control. In the nineteenth century, hygienics had taken charge of bodies and had forced them to become normalized via a collection of legal and even physical constraints. In the second half of the twentieth century, through a metamorphosis in the nature of domination (as Foucault put it, a "microphysics of power"), we witnessed an evolution toward societies of control. Constraint was now exercised with less coercion and more constancy, in a more discrete manner that was both more pernicious and more effective as it delegated control to the individuals themselves (intracontrol) and enabled the generalization of control between individuals (intercontrol). Our eyes, therefore, to continue with our cross-sectioning of the human body, made us the overseers of one another, whether this meant distributing information, denouncing our neighbors, flipping through a catalog of potential sexual partners, or sharing an entertaining video. Let us continue our descent into Gulliver's controlled body. The arms and the legs lead us to the question of muscular mass, directly linked to the democratization of the workout, even to the general injunction toward athletic performance as a mode of preventative management of excess weight, but also as a model of individual fulfillment in a stressed-out society, and even as a managerial model applied to the body (in terms of its productivity, increased power, and position within a hierarchy). In order to succeed, not only must we have a healthy body, but we must also have a fulfilling sex life. Incidentally, using our cellphones to measure our heartbeats and the number of steps we take during our morning jog means we are less available to the idea and to the practice of social change. There is also an energetic calculation to this. Energy invested in sports is energy that is taken away from all direct socio-political forms of action. The economic upsurge of the "sweat merchants" through the spread of gyms occurred parallel to the prohibition of political violence, when it did not redirect it with the more recent democratization of these gyms.

Clearly, neoliberalism is in no way a form of laissez-faire market operations and even less a form of control's slacking off. In reality, it imposes the direct and total management of the body and of the mind through a dynamic biopolitics that is certainly much less deadly than in totalitarian regimes but whose radical principle is not that distant from the way these operate. Let's continue our movement through the body, going down to the stomach this time. For a long time now, agribusiness has occupied a major economic role, and has also shaped behavior. We are now in a battle, which has become official, between fast food and slow food, organic and industrial farming, gluten-free degrowth and hamburgers for all. For some, palm oil and gluten are the number one tools of capitalist domination, such that being vegan and eating organic have become the first ingredients for future emancipation. Although there is no doubt that industrial food is worse for the planet and for our lives than locally sourced vegetables, it is clear that emancipatory movements also call for the control of ourselves and others.

If we continue this tour through our Gulliver's body, we arrive at the sex organs, which might just be the epicenter of this biopolitical mutation. Reproductive sexuality has been upended by the development of assisted reproductive technology (ART), the spectacular boom of which lies behind the fact that today one child out of seven in Europe and in the United States is born via ART. Once again, the question is not whether we should be for or against this. On the one hand, access to reproduction for homosexual couples, for example, has the political advantage of denaturalizing repro-duction, and of finally dissociating it from the heteronormative family. But, on the other, the possibility that everyone (people who are infer-tile, older couples, the sick …) can have access to the holy grail of having children is overdetermined by a logic of consumption or of market democracy according to which everyone's fulfillment is now possible and can only occur through the perpetuation of our individual lives—in the absence of larger horizons or more collective projects. We remember the dark pronouncement of the French writer Louis-Ferdinand Céline: "love is the infinite placed within the reach of poodles." This time it is parental love.

From now on, industrial laboratories, multimillionaire corporations, and bioethical laws and committees are present everywhere on our omni-surveilled bodies, and in an even more concentrated way in our ovaries and testicles. As for nonprocreative sexuality, women's magazines and dating sites, new norms, and renewed sexologies have colonized it, slipping in between our sheets every night. Let us return here to Michel Foucault's strong critique of the idea of "sexual liberation," which implied that a *good* sexuality might exist naturally, prior to being corseted by bad repressive norms.[6] He noted that from 1976 onward there was simply a shift from one system of normative practices to another. And this passage was quite spectacular, in fact. We moved from the prior, clearly prohibitive system of the Christian era to the bourgeois period's simply restrictive, semi-puritan, and partly cynical one—and finally, since the pioneering conquests of the 1960s and 1970s, to the normative, incentivizing, and even compulsory system of a fulfilled sexuality that has become the crossroads of contemporary subjectivity and the site of unprecedented malaise. The norm (which is now difficult to escape) can be clearly stated: "Your life is not successful unless you have a satisfying and fulfilled sex life at twenty-five and at sixty-five."

Finally, the economic stakes of sexuality are of course essential, with women's magazines, behavioral sexology, a whole slew of prescribed assistive protocols (Viagra, for example), and, more than ever, pornography. These are all hegemonic powers controlling and molding our pleasure by defending an essentially coital sexuality and a backward heterocentrism (despite thirty years of gay pride). They assert a principle of sexual performance obsessed with virility that produces much more sexual misery than fulfillment. The resurgence of homophobia throughout the world might be related to these new norms, which, under the cover of liberation, have revealed themselves perfectly reactionary as well. Same-sex marriage remains a necessary conquest in terms of minority rights, partly in view of the fact that its very principle still earns the ire of all conservatives—as seen with Proposition 8 in California or the ultrareactionary movement of La Manif pour Tous (The Protest for Everyone) in France. But it represents an internal normative shift within homosexual culture rather than emancipation as such. Here, we should remember the audacities of the 1970s after the Stonewall Riots, audacities that would be unthinkable today. There was the birth of gay activism in 1969 in New York, but also radical proposals such as Guy Hocquenghem's Front Homosexuel d'Action Révolutionnaire (Homosexual Front for Revolutionary Action) that began in France long before the devastation of AIDS and renormalization. The idea was not to offer a mirror image of heterosexual identity, which could finally be thought and thus criticized, but rather to propose a much more libertarian polysexuality without borders. Reinstituting legal and normative coupledom at the very site where a revolutionary expansion of the range of the "usages of pleasure" had occurred not long ago (to again use Foucault's terms) might indeed constitute legal progress, but it is not a revolution in mores. The gay world is becoming heteronormative, whereas it might have been better if the heterosexual majority had become more homosexual.

It seems that in every instance the legislator has settled in between us, in the intimacy of our crumpled sheets, from marriage equality to the proper dosage of stimulants and the necessary repression of the daily occurrences of sexual harassment. This new sexual intrusion of the law, which has come to meddle in our intimacy and in all of our interactions, is one element of the greater shift to the right. This is not because of its ethical content, since defending minorities and checking the abuse of power are rather left-wing principles; rather, the law replaced the autonomous subject of the emancipatory drive with a heteronomous superego guided by the law and by control. To end our journey through the body at the feet, we can recall here that beyond the arena of sports, hiking and adventure are now commonplace models for personal fulfillment, and that mobility and nomadism belong to contemporary managerial ideology where they function as normative obligations: Who wouldn't benefit from changing their life, their city, their neighborhood, their desk? Moving is universally recommended. Yesterday, moving was a way to shake up conservatism or to get your mind blown in Kathmandu. Today it is a way to get rid of excess fat, or to start a new professional life in another city or country. "Inertia is death": this is the formula that the new biopolitical norms incessantly repeat in the service of business downsizing, travel agents, or steroid salesmen.

From the head to the feet, a very simple idea unifies this new biopolitics and the integral management of life and bodies that it advocates for. With the aid of pills and coaches, diets and the media, we all must aspire to produce the best version of ourselves, to be a complete entrepreneur of the self, an efficient body and an adventurous spirit with a full and productive existence, who is concerned with trying everything as long as it is recommended—in the most classical sense of liberal doctrine. From this point of view, we should recognize that the Internet was not a real game-changer. It actually followed in the footsteps of a long-standing era, the half-century of vast ideological conversion that imposed individual fulfillment and self-realization, that enjoined us to lead a liberated life and to have intense experiences as a "pragmatic paradox"—that is, as the double bind of an extolled freedom and the obligation to prove it. It's a bit like those authoritarian theater instructors who demand spontaneity from their students. After all, the success of social networks is mostly due to the neoliberal obligation of a hyper-narcissistic mise-en-scène of the self and to the supposedly friendly generalized rivalry that underlies it. Andy Warhol saw a measly fifteen minutes of fame, or its promise, as the most wide-spread thing in the world. He died just before the Internet made it a definite reality for all of us.

Organized resistance to this neoliberal biopolitical program has been limited. One of the crucial fronts was comprised of groups for the defense of people with AIDS, most importantly ACT UP, founded in New York in 1987 and arriving in France in 1989. AIDS activist groups remain decisive for the struggles to come. Such groups were set up to enable people who had become infected to act on their condition, and attempted to limit the power of the pharmaceutical industry. AIDS, which at the height of the epidemic was the worst human tragedy of the time in terms of the number of victims and the "great fear" it engendered, was also the theater of a major biopolitical battle. First, an unknown disease appeared that primarily affected the homosexual community and immediately provoked an outburst of homophobia. Then, in the early 1990s, when pharmaceutical laboratories were beginning to look for cures, truly biopolitical stakes emerged. Who would control the survival of those individuals with the disease? Would it be the medical profession, industry players, the patients themselves, or the world of activists and nonprofits? The expressed demand to have mastery and autonomy over one's life—even more so, over one's critically ill body—was a new social fact with the potential to reconfigure relations of power in the public sphere. Organizations such as AIDES[7] and ACT UP fought so that the daily management of the disease could be controlled in part by the patients themselves, or by their representatives, in an equitable dialogue with the medical profession. They pioneered new forms of struggle that other groups would mimic in the years to come for other issues—the defense of illegal immigrants, for example, or unemployment advocacy. Streaks of fake blood flung across buildings or activists lying on the street as symbolic embodiments of victims ("die-ins") were not simply gimmicks to raise the visibility of protests, but were a means of renewing the modalities and the meaning of political action. No longer did activists simply aim to demand a right, but they actively struggled to maintain control over their lives (and survival). And this was the first time in decades that a pioneering political initiative had emerged in public space from the grassroots, led by the weakest element of the social body, members of a minority that was discriminated against and afflicted by a deadly virus.

Finally, the Uber model that is generalizing itself today is perhaps putting the finishing touches on this neoliberal biopolitical program. The "Uberization" of our lives can be understood as the latest advance of this all-out offensive to expand the logic of neoliberalism to all aspects of life. But, in another sense, Uber constitutes an extremely ambiguous phenomenon that is still very difficult to grasp, similar to websites that facilitate vacation rentals between individuals (Airbnb) or even that enable the geolocalized optimization of hookups (Tinder). On the one hand, Uber provides an unprecedented economic form that offers, if not emancipation, at least added revenue or savings that can sometimes be essential for precarious or poor workers—like those high-school teachers who become drivers as soon as they have some free time. And following the purest market logic, the system frees consumers from weighty additional charges by offering a taxi service at a lower price than professionals would. But that is also a biopolitical extension of neoliberal omnieconomism, which is even more pernicious than the mechanisms exerted on the different parts of our bodies. From now on, time itself has been reframed by the imperative of profitability. Just as pleasure and experience must be optimized, and sterility and solitude must stop being obstacles, it is out of the question for nonproductive time to escape the imperatives of profit. Uberization is the ultimate stage of the biopolitical conquest. The economy, in addition to capturing real time, is now also capturing possible time.

Among the fundamental partitions of the modern age that are being undone today is the opposition between free time and labor time, or, more precisely, between unproductive and productive time. This also explains why individuals are unavailable for collective protest. Far from the Stalinist dictatorships, the time when communism in Western Europe drew a third of the electorate was also a time when Sundays weren't reserved for going to mass or for updating your blogs, but for ritual protests of collective self-affirmation. Behind

the stupidities of dogma and the lies of the oligarchs, these protests also served an emancipative
cause and a need for social community. If I drive a
car or constantly update my Facebook page, my
self-affirmation will be neither political nor collective. These kinds of changes also render the debates
over the reduction of labor time a bit ridiculous,
since labor and survival (or "overwork," as Marx
would say) have invaded the entirety of our lives
far beyond office hours. This colonization of free
time affects all levels of work. Senior executives are
also trapped by a system of generalized rivalry that
makes them available at will—or, should we say,
"Uberizable" by their boss. But the idea is not to
pity the fortunate ones in the new class struggle.
It's better to be bothered by your boss when you
are on a beach in Costa Rica with your family than
not to be able to afford vacation at all.

3. The Foreclosure of Conflict

In the face of such evolutions, individual or collective resistance is not easy. Refusal, whether passive
or offensive, has grown more rare, and isolates
those who dare to engage in it. In this sense, there
are two elements that combine to form the black
box or the secret knot of this swing to the right of
the last forty years. On the one hand is the extension of the market to all aspects of life, and on the

other, although inseparably, is what psychoanalysis calls the "foreclosure of conflict"—that is, the prohibition and repression of the contentious nature not only of social relations but also of time and of existence in general. An entire contentious dimension is thus both encompassed and obscured by an unprecedented and systematic violence, the violence of precarity and competition presented as natural and inevitable. Conflict has become inconceivable and impracticable. The four decades in question are mostly defined by this foreclosure of conflict. This is the period when conflict becomes largely unthinkable and is always already contained. It takes places within structures and subjectivities, but is strictly regulated, even prohibited, in the space of collective power relations. Conflict, which has shifted into structures and has become euphemized and objectified within the system itself, is thus rendered invisible and impossible to deconstruct. Conflict, in the sense of the deliberate domination that is being denied everywhere as well as the active resistance that could oppose it, is dehistoricized and naturalized.

As we were saying above, there is no need to maintain the terms "right" and "left" today. If we do decide to keep them, given that their doctrinal contents are now hazy or diluted, we can simply associate with what used to be called the Left the notion of "conflict" and of "taking on conflict." If

the Left is to stand for anything other than a misleading management or a deceptive heritage, it
should stand for the possibility of conflict, the
possibility of opposing social injustice and the
macrostructures of power with both words and
actions. This opposition can no longer be conceived, even up to the cult references of the new
struggles. Take, for example, the unanimous
reading of Henry David Thoreau's celebrated text
Civil Disobedience as a manifesto of nonviolence.[8]
This is not the case. Thoreau's early nineteenth-
century idol was James Brown, the mythic hero who
inspired Quentin Tarantino's *Django Unchained*, a
former black slave who rebelled and killed dozens
of white slaveholders. In his text, Thoreau
explained very clearly that when the laws in place
contradict our personal and collective sense of
justice, it is our duty to disobey. This form of disobedience—which can be violent or nonviolent,
and has at its disposal a vast repertoire of actions—
constitutes what I am calling "conflict."

Conflict has also always been a democratic necessity. Saint-Just and Thomas Jefferson were already
saying this at the end of the eighteenth century:
enemy blood must flow for the roots of the democratic tree to grow. No one says this anymore. The
discussion now centers on the necessary limits of
democratic conflict. Contradiction is only soluble in
negotiation, according to the liberal theorists of

democracy for the last forty years. This is one aspect, although only one aspect, of the "communicative rationality" theorized by the German philosopher Jürgen Habermas and founded on the "ethics of discussion"—a concept that is much richer than we think, but that has been diverted by the ideologues of representative democracy or by high-profile moralists. In fact, the foreclosure and naturalization of conflict has taken multiple forms during these last four decades. First, there was that great technocratic Western fantasy, found in the mass media as well as in the discourse of trendy young politicians in the early 1980s, of overcoming the right/left, progressive/conservative polarity, considered old-fashioned and counterproductive, in favor of a government of experts working *objectively* for the good of all. This entelechy of expertise, defended by Washington think tanks or by the Saint-Simon Foundation in France, held out the pipe dream of a government of the competent. A similar idea emerging at the time was the idea of a "centrist government, or of a "Republic of the Center."[9] Behind the appearance of conflict upheld to justify their democratic election, the political forces involved were in reality ideologically interchangeable and foregrounded their technical competence to occupy an absent center, aspiring to institutional convergence. This artificial construction of the left/right polarity existed in the United

States as well, at least until the spectacular turn of events of Trump's election. The institutional networks of both parties, from legal experts to lobbyists, remained formally separate but agreed on the basics. In the US, in Europe, and in the large emerging countries reigned the lie of overcoming politics through the advent of experts. The crisis of political representation and of the collective adhesion that it had garnered for a long time was not primarily the consequence of the discrediting of the political class; it was, rather, the effect of this rise to power of experts. The career of an expert, whether they are an overcredentialed advisor or an arrogant technocrat, a "specialist" media subscriber or an influential director of a think tank, can be summarized as a long fight against politics, against its commitments, its polarities, its affects, and its symbolic autonomy. As the constant reference for all power, experts are never elected, never responsible, and their yapping sows doubt in the mind of electors. What use is voting if politics consists of decisions made by experts?

A second striking symptom of this foreclosure of conflict is how euphemized dominant language has become. Media discourse, or that of politicians and business leaders, skirts the realities of social relations and international relations. It no longer calls a spade a spade. As the case may be, a war can be called a "surgical strike" or a "humanitarian intervention." Someone who is unemployed is someone who is "seeking employment." The eviction of thousands of workers is called "restructuring," the dogged struggle to win over one's rivals is "self-fulfillment," etc. If we follow the evolution of vocabulary, this transformation of signifiers (and of the perceptions inherent in them) began as early as the 1970s–80s. This was a long time before the appearance of "political correctness" at the turn of the 1990s, a way of euphemizing language that had the virtuous intentions of trying to reduce social suffering and discrimination, and to recognize minorities in language that did not add to the scars of historical violence. Here, we are instead evoking the performative syntax of dominant language as it evacuates the contentious aspect of social facts and transforms people into things, instances of violence into structures, and situations into inevitabilities. In a few decades, the poor have become "marginalized," bums have become "homeless," immigrants who have been arrested by the police are "illegal aliens," the economic devastation of entire sectors or regions is a "restructuring," etc. We should reread German linguist Viktor Klemperer's daily diary analyzing the syntax of the Third Reich as he was trying to survive the Nazi storm. There, we find the same gap between the violence of lived experience and the objectifying hypocrisy of the words used to describe it. In the case of neoliberalism, this discursive layer (which we no longer notice) allows ideas and economic and social realities to be painted in ways that render them indisputable, ordinary, and acceptable—at once, both distanced and normalized. This metamorphosis of language has greatly contributed to the removal of the possibility of conflict.

The *soft power* of this new language is relentless. In it, everything is linked: the extension of managerial control, the euphemizing of discourse, the commercial homogenization of speech, false signifiers—plus the lexical globalization of English, or Globish, under the aegis of American global hegemony, with the concurrent cultural impoverishment of all languages and of their specificities. Entrepreneurial Newspeak, to use George Orwell's term, has terribly reduced our vocabularies. In the United States, the reaction to managerial logorrhea has even led to an entertaining bingo game, played during business meetings, which consists in checking off field-specific jargon as well as recurrent general expressions: "best practices," "going forward," "paradigm shift," "equity" (included as a reasonable alternative to "equality" …), "growth," "circle back," "bandwidth," "community managers," "turnover," etc. The first person to successfully check off all the words stands and cries, "Bullshit bingo!" This is a liberating game. It reminds us that our very syntax is full of discrete discursive operators that orient our vision of the world and block any logical possibility for conflict or resistance. When employees (or precarious workers) and bosses (or stakeholders) who are structural adversaries are designated in the public sphere as "social partners," the simple idea that they are in conflict disappears.

The third, even greater symptom of this foreclosure of conflict is the systematic individualization of social and collective questions. Environmental issues, for example, which imply planetary responsibilities, mass interests, and political decisions, are presented via the angle of personal commitment and individual failings, when those who are primarily responsible for the ecological disaster are the large industrial groups. In the same way, the macroeconomic questions linked to layoffs and to deindustrialization are only treated from the point of view of the individual efforts necessary to overcome them, or in terms of personal narratives around the loss of social position. Cases of "burn out" are emblematic. The collective and therefore social dimension of the phenomenon of extreme pressure at work is never mentioned in media coverage. Instead, the media treats "burn out" as a work-related accident or an individual's bad luck.

Finally, whether it happens through the fantasy of dissolving politics into expertise, through the usage of language, or with the individualization of problems, conflict is evaded via a cultural stratum, a directly ideological discursive layer. For this prohibition-disappearance of conflict goes hand in glove with the extension of culture and its endless discourse at the expense of history and politics. By substituting successive change in our visions of the world with instantaneous plurality—in other words, by replacing space with time and culture with politics—social transformation has been rendered inconceivable. From now on, the world is seen as a juxtaposition of different points of view that will hopefully grant a place to each minority. This juxtaposition in space has replaced the previous vision of an open temporal axis inscribed in a dialectical movement, under the influence of materialism and Marxism, but also of historicism and of the political willpower of the liberal elites of the twentieth century. When social change is replaced by the foregrounding of cultural differences that have been essentialized and dehistoricized, welcomed and decontextualized—rather than articulating both things and thinking the question of minorities in conjunction with the issue of general struggle—the very possibility of social conflict is removed. In France, for example, such essentializing culturalism, which is good-hearted in journalistic antiracism but much more marginalizing in editorial Islamophobia, has simply widened the gap between what is considered legitimate and the real situation on the ground, and between the false debates on TV shows and the feeling of disempowerment (and even of unexpressed anger) on the part of minorities. A gulf divides France—between between the anticommunitarian republicanism of the elites, who hold onto a logic that is itself centered on identity (white, Judeo-Christian, Western-centric), and a postcolonial France that is alive and kicking but has been rendered invisible. Making up nearly 30% of the population, and not restricted to people living in underprivileged neighborhoods, this France remains almost totally absent from public space.

Here, the term "culturalism" designates the fact that only cultural difference is taken into account, generally in a complimentary way, to the exclusion of all other differences. This leads to the representation of culture (itself a vague mix of historical references, religions, languages, rites, and ordinary practices) as a natural characteristic that is unchangeable and overdetermining. The dominant culturalists are incapable of thinking the part played by strategy in dictating cultural affirmation—the game of masks that is essential to the survival of minorities—as well as the complex historical construction of identities and their representations. They make a mistake in reasoning that a child would not make. Identity as a space in which relative positions are possible should not be confused with identity understood as the imperative of permanent secession. It's not because people have another culture, other daily practices, and that they speak a different language that they refuse to integrate into the more or less abstract entity, "society" or "nation," in which they live. But conservatives are not the only ones to oppose communitarian culture and participation in society as a whole without taking into account the dialectic synergy between the two: we find the same mistake in the unitary logic of both the social and extreme Left inherited from the twentieth century. Especially in Europe, this enabled the development of an implicit colonial racism and a white-national imperialism at the heart of these movements, and rendered invisible sexual or ethnic minorities. And in the United States, when leftwing intellectuals criticize different minority politics for leading to the "twilight of common dreams," this same gap is being reinforced.[10]

To return to the foreclosure of conflict, within a few decades, violence in the sense of real confrontation beyond discourse has clearly disappeared as a means of collective action. Perhaps this is why it has recently become a hot potato. In France in 2015, the few trade unionists who pushed around the human resources director of Air France and tore off his nice white shirt after the surprise announcement of a job-cutting plan were described in the media as criminals, barbarians, even terrorists. A sign of the times. Violence has become generalized as a systematic fate, as the weakening of lives, and at the same time it has evaporated as an instrument of emancipation if tearing off that shirt, which went with a six-figure salary, could be considered a "barbaric" act. Today, the mathematical remainder of this curious operation is perhaps incidentally the actual violence of Islamic terrorism, which is unprecedented and spectacular but which also functions as a screen to blind, hypnotize, and stop us from considering the other forms of violence that structure the rest of our daily life. If we want to understand this long era of foreclosure of conflict, it is fundamental that we confront the question of violence. Neoliberal ideologues and mainstream historians alike often present this period as the "pacification" phase of Western societies, a time in which the political violence of the early twentieth century and the ordinary criminality of the poor were eliminated. In reality, it was mostly a phase that witnessed the normative and juridical foreclosure of violence. Violence has been transformed into a scarecrow, a misleading monolith, a bygone and impossible thing, or one that doesn't "happen to us"—contrary to the entire moral and political history of the West. Today, people have gone so far as to decree that violence against material things is as serious, in terms of jurisprudence and of public morality, as violence against people. When protesters during the 1992 Los Angeles riots destroyed public property and plundered supermarkets, or when youth in the French suburbs burned bus stops and schools in November 2005, they faced criminal charges equivalent to homicide. And pundits saw in these actions a "barbarism" they deemed as serious as deliberate massacres. Such a juridical and normative prohibition of violence is mostly a way to prevent uprisings led by social movements. It developed over the years with widespread and active complicity, even on the part of the parties belonging to the historical extreme Left, which one after the other shut the door on political violence.

These parties threw the baby out with the bathwater, and abandoned the specter of violence as a means of collective action. Spontaneous modalities of collective action that do not exclusively pertain to instituted discussion and negotiation with the powers that be—whether they be occupations, sabotages, huge protests, passive obstruction, or the physical reclaiming of land—have been rendered unthinkable. At the same time, systemic, euphemized, insidious, and structural violence has increased. Such violence is now objectively measurable by the wage gap, by subjective malaise, or by the menace of ecological apocalypse, but also by the constant exacerbation of all of these. The system has become more violent than ever. Admittedly, we no longer whip galley slaves, or send people to prison without trial. The death penalty has been banned in Europe—although it still exists in twenty-nine states in the United States—and there are perhaps less murders being committed in the streets. But we deny or underestimate suffering at work, repressed intersubjective tension, waves of suicide, and the daily distress of employees and precarious workers when these realities are more and more present at the heart of our lives. On a global scale, increasingly deadly local conflicts, intercommunitarian rivalries, and interreligious wars also function as modes of regulating systemic global violence, via catharsis or energetic release. This violence has been imposed on us in an invisible and indisputable way, while the foreclosure of the instrumental and tactical violence of social movements has also precluded the possibility of opposing it *directly*.

The aestheticized violence of special effects in action TV shows and blockbusters is steeped in this systemic violence, and it expulses it with immense pleasure. This violence seeps through these new images, where it is either reduced to its essence or inflamed, as the case may be. But people often make the mistake of establishing a direct causal link between violence in the movies or in video games and acts of violence, such as the school shootings that regularly explode in the United States. There is, however, no direct link. The real cause of this violence by adolescents who start shooting their schoolyards with assault rifles is the fantasmatic derealization of violence, as well as the availability of weapons. Violence has become an iconic phenomenon, on the order of the hologram or the pure image. It can thus take on unbelievable, even comic proportions in movies the way it did, frivolously, twenty-five years ago in the film series *Die Hard*. The festive and fictional generalization of violence at the heart of American pop culture is what finally depoliticized and dehistoricized social violence. Violence became what people do with their joysticks or in front of their screens, or what the lunatics who are recruited by the Islamic State do—this recent history of violence has been like an orgy of morbid escalations, a kind of compulsive thanatophilia.

The violence of fiction or on TV reports has a very direct effect on the derealization of the world. In order to understand the relation between real invisible violence and hystericized imaginary violence—which is to say, the relation between what little we *can* do and what we *do* do to counterbalance real violence—the work of Sigmund Freud, Herbert Marcuse, or Hannah Arendt is still very pertinent today because it belongs to an energetics of violence.[11] Structural violence and the world of lived experience, or socioeconomic and subjective conditions and daily human relations, are like communicating vessels. When our collective capacity for action has been reduced to its bare minimum, when we are constantly told that there is no alternative and that it is unthinkable to modify the rules of the game, sooner or later this logically leads to the necessary expulsion of a long-internalized violence that has been endured and repressed by individual and collective disempowerment. This belated expulsion can take three different forms: a social uprising that is more or less thought-out and judicious and aimed at a more or less identified power; the more personal form of intersubjective violence, ranging from the man who beats his wife to local phenomena of scapegoating and demonizing difference; or the cathartic form of a certain enjoyment of the death drive through the overconsumption of video games by poorly socialized adolescents or simply in nervous binge-watching of TV shows. In the first case, there is crystallization and a rallying against a nameable enemy. In the second, there is a cruel lateral diversion, from the more ordinary (domestic violence) to the more general (the rise of xenophobic discourse). The third case implies impulsive compensation, either scopic or fetishistic.

To return to the situation to which we've been led by this long, right-wing shift of nearly a half century, against a backdrop of intensifying and expanding systemic violence we must remember that the first form of expulsion of violence, the social movement in action, is the only way to limit the other two. As long as the first form of reaction, which concentrates and rationalizes refusal by designating the enemy, remains morally condemned and juridically criminalized—as is the case in the recent states of emergency imposed in France, in Turkey, and in North America—the other logics of scapegoating and impulsive catharsis, which lead to disaster, will continue to gain a foothold. It is no surprise that the contemporary terrorist violence that is so haunting draws on the three registers in its own way. Therein lies its success in seducing a few weak minds, and its impact on our imaginaries: the rhetoric of an uprising against the imperial enemy, the cathartic imputing of failings to predefined groups (Christians, Jews, Westerners, infidels, etc.), and the image of an impulsive orgy worthy of an extreme video game, with fear added. The conclusion is logical. The more we can deploy social movements, the more this kind of violence will recede. No military victory or police action can efficiently protect us from it; only the active mobilization of everyone in social struggles will reveal the existence and the autonomous power of a people.

3

COUNTERING THE RIGHT WITHOUT
SEIZING POWER?

During this time, starting at the beginning of the 1980s, the Left, or what used to be called the Left, became a ghost of itself. The sad experience of power—for the moderate Left, on the one hand, and for the radical left-wing parties (in their abandoning of collective uprisings), on the other—ended up inverting the very concept of the Left. It swapped the future for the past, and invention for safeguarding. From the extreme Left to the electoral Left, dominant leftist language shifted from deliberate change, impelled by popular uprisings or by reform, to the defense of acquired rights and resistance to change inasmuch as change has become the operative preserve of the neoliberals. Left-wing terminology has literally—although not ideologically—become *conservative*. The question now is how to *conserve* a given situation, to salvage what's left of a quickly disappearing model of a mixed, or partially redistributive, economy. Logically, the same inversion exists on the other side. The discourse of the powers on the right has gone from being principally patrimonial and reactionary, aimed at defending tradition, to a pedagogy of compulsory modernization and market enthusiasm that is only counterbalanced by a call to family and patriotic values to sweeten the pill of economic chaos. Additionally, this amalgamated Right has appropriated the critical vocabulary of the Left, its old subversive position. Unless it was simply the case that on the left this vocabulary had gone unused for so long that it became available, so that all the Right needed to do was recover it and invert its political content.

1. The End of Public Intellectuals and the Displacement of Critique

But first, the social rights that had been won in the 1960s had to be diverted toward media-market democracy, which was now advocating for tolerance, diversity, the normative permissiveness of mores, and, of course, creativity and mobility. By opposing this, reactionaries and champions of regression won over the debate. For the general public, the Right's open critique and questioning of the new normativity, in the name of Reaction, became synonymous with courage and freedom of spirit, and made the Right appear as a heroic minority in a sea of conformity … At least, this was how conservatives made their case for usurping the monopoly of critique with their so-called intellectual courage starting in the 1980s. The operation was obvious in the intellectual field, even if it remains of secondary importance. More than ever, instead of triggering evolutionary processes as some intellectuals dreamed of doing, intellectuals simply *accompanied* them. Just when critical thought ran out of steam, as if tongue-tied, conservative thought pilfered the used clothes of ostentatious indignation and of supposed bravery. "Commitment," a somewhat clichéd notion dating from the end of the Second World War, shifted utterly to the Right. Social uprisings, which had been politically disabled and morally compromised, came to occupy the role of a good ghost in intellectual discourse, and at the same time social conflicts were shifting from the site of productive relations to minority rights. Critical theory did not really have a place there, and quickly deserted the intellectual debate. The rare people who continued to practice it were beset by general indifference or by public shaming, accused by pundits of being old-fashioned or Gulag capos. We remember the vile "antitotalitarian" operation that inaugurated the great turn of the 1970s—"vile," because the discovery and condemnation of Soviet totalitarianism had occurred long before the French New Philosophers or even Aleksandr Solzhenitsyn's decisive testimony in *The Gulag Archipelago*, the earth-shaking editorial event of 1974. The exiled Leon Trotsky paid for Soviet totalitarianism with his life. David Rousset had been telling the general public about it since 1947. And the 1950s group Socialisme ou Barbarie (Socialism or Barbarism) had twenty years on the squawking of the young intellectual bourgeoisie in 1978, a handful of devious journalists and careerist essayists monopolizing the defense of Eastern dissidents and of the victims of Stalinist purges. Logically, this resulted in a *Time* magazine cover announcing "Marx is Dead," following the title of an essay one such journalist had written, epitomizing the grandiose wishful thinking of Western elites.[1] This strange second half of the 1970s was the moment when young showmen (or TV-show personalities)—who were younger than thirty, kept their shirts loosely unbuttoned, and proclaimed themselves the heirs of the Enlightenment—revisited history. It was a time when it was fashionable to attend "antitotalitarian" cocktail parties or symposia that paid tribute to Soviet dissidents. This had the immediate and lasting correlate of criminalizing any mention of communism in Western Europe. All forms of communism were flushed down the drain, from the Soviet kind (which was so far from communism) to anarchist, leftist, theoretical, trade unionist, and literary communism. This "antitotalitarian" moment was the ideal occasion, once again, to throw the baby out with the bathwater.

Purged of Marxism at the turn of the 1980s, the academy also became a shadow of itself over the next four decades, moving light years from its existence at the end of the 1960s as an enclave of critical independence (whether in the North American humanities, or in the rich experience of France's alternative university in Vincennes.) In a quarter century, the academy has become an advanced platform for "public management" and for the neoliberal utilitarianism of "useful" knowledge (the new "knowledge economy" that is so ill-named). In ten years, the academy's previously held positions were aggressively marginalized. Critical sociology was pushed out in favor of methodological individualism and North American interactionism; social history was often replaced by cultural history; and, of course, management and microeconomics replaced yesterday's political economy. This also happened to philosophy, in the broad sense of the word, which left the terrain of modern critical thinking—that vast continent ranging from the Freudian-Marxism of the early twentieth century (notably, the Frankfurt School), to the left-wing Nietzscheanism of the second half of the twentieth century (Foucault, Deleuze, Lyotard, et al.)—in favor of a new neo-Kantian moralism. In the United States, critical theory ceded to a liberal neopragmatism; more recently, academic philosophy has become reenchanted with good old metaphysics, a turn that has sometimes been made to serve the neurosciences and technological posthumanism.

Such changes were a sign of the times. The "modern" academy had to stop being so uncool and forego political commitments that were deemed obsolete, along with the retrograde references associated with them. These changes can also be explained by the personal strategies and the institutional successes of a few anti-Marxist barons. But they were also an effect of the economic crisis. With the rise in unemployment, students opted for curricula that would lead to jobs by turning to law, economics, communication, or the hard sciences. Since the human and social sciences attracted fewer students, their professors were more limited. As Gilles Deleuze used to say in 1980—almost as if to apologize for *A Thousand Plateaus*, the UFO he was launching at the time with Félix Guattari, quite against the grain—critique was no longer in the spirit of the times. From this point of view, the inaugural symbolic event of that period was the forced evacuation of the prefab campus of Vincennes by the antiriot police in 1979, under the pretext of stopping drug trafficking and incitement to violence. Smoking joints and doing Lacanian psychoanalysis have never been such threats to the social order!

The end of the twentieth century also saw the disappearance, one after the other, of the great figures of critical thought born after the war—from Roland Barthes, who died in 1980, to Jacques Derrida, who died in 2004, to focus simply on the French thinkers who'd been made *stars* for a time on the other side of the Atlantic. This was another objective aspect of the taming of the intellectual field. Yet this idea of the "end of the great thinkers" is more complex than it seems, and cannot be reduced to a few individual obituaries. A first factor behind the disappearance of the great critical intellectuals was the modification of the public space of ideas that had become, over the course of a few years, an industrial site for the production of best-selling essays and formatted debates for the new audio-visual scene, with authors whose first requirement was to excel on TV shows and to break with liberal narrow-mindedness on hip talk-shows. The second factor, which we've already mentioned, was the individual opportunism of a few of these figures. The story of post-1968 trajectories full of about-faces and backpedaling is now well known. People ranging from the New Left pioneer David Horowitz to French ex-Maoist André Glucksmann—or the likes of Irving Kristol, a former Trotskyist who founded *The National Interest* and defined a neo-conservative as "a liberal who has been mugged by reality"—pulled it off perfectly after they'd exorcized the "red devil" who had supposedly possessed them in their early youth. They entered life with that certificate of good conduct, and are still at the forefront of the scene forty years later.

This initial operation of exorcizing the leftist virus explains the longevity of these figures. All of those who so ostensibly "came back to their right mind"—that is, to liberal reason and to counterutopian pseudorealism, by shifting from a revolutionary position (that was often very rhetorical) to an erudite reformist or conservative posture—made their "youthful error" the very example of what not to do. This became the moral base of a certain model of life, and the source of their legitimacy. By means of a strange parallel, we could even compare these examples of extreme redemptive shifts with the notorious Monica Lewinsky case that made such big headlines at the end of the 1990s in the United States. After the phase of media obsession over the semen stain and oral sex in the Oval Office, not only was President Clinton not impeached, but his approval rating returned thanks to the staging of his sin and its purging, just like a Baptist who offers up his own depravity as a sacrifice to enable collective redemption: "I sinned; therefore, you are absolved." In another context, we find the same approach taken by those who went from the Mao suit to the

Rotary Club, and who turned this passage into proof of their credibility. It's as if they were saying: "I forbid you to join the revolution; we did and we know what it brings." In other words, "I sinned in the past and my sin absolves you; thanks to me, you will remain innocent and pure for eternity."

Another factor we've seen is a general prohibition of all critical thought through populist pressure on public opinion and the systematic bleeding of the great institutions of knowledge. We should add another, more ambiguous, factor that says more about the crisis of the great public intellectuals than that of critical thought itself: the objective democratization of intellectual life. In all Western countries, the fact that eighty percent of an entire generation had access to higher education, combined with the overproduction of PhDs and books in the humanities, as well as the digital revolution and the easy access to knowledge that it enabled, produced a generation that is today overinformed, overerudite, and sometimes even overcritical, but excessively disempowered. The need for gurus to critique the ruling order has disappeared, and we will need many more resources than those of the intellectual field to begin to transform it. We can say anything, criticize everything, and think everything, but the horizons of protest action are much smaller. In a sense, it is easier to say no than to *do* no. In the face of such democratization of the fields of knowledge, which is also very good news, there is no doubt that master public intellectuals remain necessary, especially in France where there is an old tradition of brown-nosing leading intellectual figures, but also in the American academy, where showcasing and competition between campuses encourages an intellectual star system and faculty careerism. Yet such figures are more difficult to impose. In the end, people are less easily taken in.

The other essential factor that helps explain the end of the great critical figures and the generation gap in the field of ideas is the professionalization and specialization of intellectual work. Serious intellectuals left the public arena, for they no longer had their place in the logic of entertainment and moral blackmail that rules over TV, where Glenn Beck replaced Carl Bernstein a long time ago. But today, on the other hand, the doctrinal and internal hyperspecialization of academic knowledge, all the more so in the humanities, produces excellent technicians of literary analysis, cutting-edge specialists in the history of philosophy, and experts in social theory limited to their single field of expertise and to the exclusivity of the scientific community. It is as if hyperspecialization in the academic world is an effect of government by experts and the ideology of expertise, generally. A final, essential factor is the self-criticism of intellectual power. For behind the diversity of forms of thought exhibited by this generation of critical intellectuals—that of Barthes, Foucault, Derrida, Deleuze, and Lévi-Strauss, to stay in the domain of French theory—these thinkers shared an ethical resistance to their own influence, a way to saw the branch on which they were seated and to deconstruct the very bedrock of intellectual power, rendering the figure of the master impossible and denouncing the artificial hierarchies of the academic world. They refused the master status that was belatedly attributed to them and declined to gather around themselves a doctrine and a group of followers—sometimes, they nearly asserted that they didn't care what happened after they were gone. When the late Foucault was giving conferences in the United States before thousands of people and received questions from the public that were increasingly existential or spiritual, concerning the meaning of life or how to live well, he would get more and more annoyed and assert that he wasn't there to tell them how to live. When we compare this attitude to the current success of media opinion-makers with their moral prescriptions, or New Age philosophies that purport to be therapeutic in selling watered-down versions of ancient techniques of the self, the epochal shift from Chomsky to "positive thinking," or from Foucault to talk-show debates, is immediately apparent.

We could consider this a good thing, after all, and wish for the great figures of critical thought to be replaced with a more autonomous generation, more grassroots critical practices, and collective intellectuals. But we are not there yet. The idea of the collective intellectual still comes up against a number of obstacles. The publishing industry is based on the logic of the single author, as are notions of copyright and the entire media industry. And yet, far from TV sets and marketing strategies, this idea has been slowly gaining ground over the past twenty years, ever since the nonprofit world and the new social movements have integrated a whole field of intellectual work into their struggle and their strategies for autonomy: collective readings, popular education, debates on activist social networks, the unpacking of legal texts, and open invitations to sociologists and philosophers to come share their knowledge on the ground. From ACT Up, the American branch of the Earth Liberation Front, British Deep Ecology, and the young combatants of France's Zone à Défendre (Zones to Defend) who improvised against airport or dam projects, to the informal collectives of the alter-globalization movement at the turn of the millennium (Attac, Reclaim the Streets, etc.) and Occupy Wall Street, all of these function more or less as true collective intellectuals, "collective agencies of enunciation," as Deleuze and

Guattari would say. They have tactics for counter-interpretation, activist libraries, collective readings, and more or less well-established conceptual apparatuses, but they do not have representatives or an authorial name, and they therefore do not have great notoriety or access to the dominant media.

And if they have reemerged since the end of the 1990s, these spread-out collectives dedicated to particular causes and to radical critique don't carry much weight in the face of the great return, in the dominant discourse, of the myth of the nation and of the endangered homeland. The nation, the first of the modern political signifiers that went from the Left to the Right, from the popular uprisings of the nineteenth century to the xenophobic extremisms of the twentieth, has recolonized the public space of debate and ideas, and the ambient political discourse—whether it is America that is either "back" (Reagan) or "great again" (Trump), or whether it is every European country orchestrating its own national reenchantment via fetishized historical heritage or essentialized history. National and heritage-based right-wing historicism, which was brought to power by Reagan and Trump in the United States, and by Nicolas Sarkozy in France, is also antisocial. The very term "historicism" implies that the period of social change, that long era of social uprising and of revolution as a political objective that began at the end of the eighteenth century, has definitively ended. It was nothing more than a historical parenthesis that lasted a bit less than two centuries. Things are now back to normal, back to the cycles of political power and to the narratives of battles, of heroes, and of changes in mores. The history of the winners, as Foucault used to call it—that is, the history of great men, of military events, and of the eternal Nation—became omnipresent, reassuring, democratized. We would have to wait for the turn of the new millennium for a pluralistic history, even a history "from the bottom," and for a critical revision of the colonial question—excavated here and there in all of the countries that had repressed it for so long—to finally gain access to public space. But this remained on the margins, and was not without fierce polemics.

In the same way, after decades of methodological individualism and a proudly positive functionalism in the social sciences, more critical avenues have recently opened. Dominant epistemologies have been dismantled on the side of postcolonial perspectives, or with the critique of the new forms of the neoliberal police state and its securitarian buildup. And let's not forget the promising innovations that are connected to history, to counterfactual history, and to subaltern history, approaches which are still marginal but very inspiring and which provide sites for a critical view. There are critical scholars, but so few positions to anchor them in the institution, and few echoes of their research at the heart of public space. But, in general, we should put this misery of the intellectual world in perspective. The intellectual world is not a leader for the rest of society. Let us be more Maoists than Confucians. History is never made with ideas, with discursive strategies or through their intellectual producers, but via the complex game of power relations. What happened after the 1970s in the intellectual field, the erosion of critical thought and the sudden prohibition of Marxist or alternative epistemologies, was simply a local consequence of a much larger crisis of the political and activist Left, a crisis that affected the Left in its very principle, and the different leftist movements in their plurality. It is important to evoke the stages of this crisis, to describe its modalities but also the most recent signs of awakening, in order to understand why it sometimes seems as though there isn't much resistance to the world shift to the right—that is, the historical alliance of an anarcho-hysterical market economy, at once biopolitical and libidinal, with the conservative and securitarian backlash that is everywhere apparent. In the face of this, left-wing groups are more than ever in crisis, caught between renunciation, awakening, disempowerment, and melancholy.

2. The Left, from Denial to Awakening

But we should speak of different "lefts," for there are two divergent aspects according to which left we are considering. On the one hand, there is the disappearance of the political Left, via its convergence with the dominant institutional and economic apparatuses, once it gains power. On the other, we have an implosion/metamorphosis of the critical Left that inherited the different leftist movements of the 1960s and shifts its objects and roles. For this critical Left, we have to take into account the long process spanning the 1970s–80s, during which the revolutionary project was abandoned—with the foregoing of political violence and even, more generally, with the discarding of activist mobilization as an aim in itself. This just disappeared. We know the story. It begins with radicalization, then rupture, then self-dissolution on all fronts, and soon enough people end up abandoning the struggle. In the United States, the SDS was dissolved as early as 1969, divided between the Marxist-Leninist minority (the Progressive Labor group) and the majority that was closer to the struggle for civil rights. In France, 1973 saw the dissolution of the Maoist Gauche Prolétarienne (Proletarian Left) and of the Trotskyist Ligue Communiste Révolutionnaire (Revolutionary Communist League). There was the headlong rush toward extreme-left terrorism in Italy and Germany, which had more or less broken away from its social base, and with the Weathermen in America, when Nixon decided to invade Cambodia. The end was there from the very beginning: between their forced clandestinity, the obsession with self-dissolution, and the deliberate isolation of cells that sought to form clandestine avant-guards rather than to federate, these kinds of extreme-left microcellular groups were quickly driven to disappear. Additionally, all of this was happening against a background of economic crisis that demoralized activist youth, and was topped off by the moralizing campaigns of the antitotalitarian movement that finally discredited the Left in the face of public opinion.

To add to all this, the notion of social class that provided the key to the "unitary" mobilization of radicals on the left was progressively erased. For, although the class struggle was perhaps even more violent under Thatcher or Reagan than it had been twenty years earlier, everything combined to distance or obscure class *consciousness*, beginning with the erosion of its old conduits. The notion of class disappeared from explanatory tools, from situational analyses, and from the references of those who were the first concerned. And yet its antagonistic power was clearly there, without safeguards. For de-Marxization also implied the rapid forfeiting of those pillars of electoral communism: popular education, political economy explained to all, and a whole pedagogical and institutional awakening of class consciousness. All of this was erased over the course of a few years with the electoral—and therefore, financial and institutional—decline of the extreme-left parties in Europe. This decline was particularly evident for the Communist Party, but could also be seen in the decline of the Left and its headlong rush toward power, in the prohibition of dialectical and historical approaches in public discourse, or in the deceleration of social change. The very notion of social class was censored, deemed scientifically inadequate, as were the concepts of struggle and of class consciousness. During the 1980s and 1990s, a number of management gurus and a new breed of positive sociologists claimed to demonstrate that classes as historically constituted social entities were being replaced by "lifestyles" that one could (almost) freely choose. In France, the "socio-styles" that were showcased by the guru-consultant Bernard Cathelat in magazines at the time classified society into stylistic "tribes" and "families." Trend forecasting in the United States divided society into lifestyles based on the postulate of the *homo economicus* and his much-discussed rational choices. People were classified as hip, show-off, austere, spendthrift, prudent, etc. Anything was possible in terms of definitions, as long as defined social positions could be replaced by supposed aesthetic choices and behaviors, and by existentially coded, strictly individual strategies, as if all of this just happened by magic and was not anchored in any social ground. This was a truly unbelievable slippage. Regardless of the scientific value of these "socio-styles," there was no doubt that the terms in question no longer had anything to do with social classes and could therefore not constitute their historical "replacement."

After the end of the 1970s, social scientists who were more openly on the left also made ecology, feminism, and issues around identity or culture into substitutes for prior social movements, claiming the latter had stifled and homogenized them. They were pitting one against the other, minority singularities against activists, whereas ten years before, during the civil rights struggle or May 1968, these themes had been inextricable. Very rapidly, precise and specific issues such as environmental vigilance or gender parity would be detached from that great belief in social change and integrated into the dominant politics so as to give it some soul, and ideological surplus value. By the time so-called real communism suddenly crumbled like a house of cards at the end of 1989, the dice had already long been cast. In fact, the major blow against the idea of revolution did not occur with the fall of the Berlin Wall and the dismantling of the Eastern Bloc, which opened up markets and often perpetuated the stronghold of mafia oligarchs, but with the official interpretation given to this event by the Western media and ideologues. Whatever had defined the social movement or even simply the Left for the prior two centuries, from a redistributive state to council communism, had to be completely forgotten. End of discussion. At least during the several years when no critical voices were raised, these ideologues kept hammering home that one day or another it all led to political prisons or to grotesque Stalinism. The process was simply inevitable, like a fact of nature, and that was how it was. There was therefore no other choice, once again, but to throw out the baby of social critique with the bathwater of historical communism.

Intellectuals and the critical Left thus found themselves in a period of mourning, an enforced mourning for a terminology that had become suspect and a more internal mourning for a certain collective desire for general emancipation that had suddenly been prohibited. From then on, for a good decade, revolution and social change would become specters, or zombie concepts that were neither fully attested nor truly dead. This was the point of departure for Jacques Derrida's book *Specters of Marx*, which Marxists hated.[2] It is impossible to say whether specters, like the characters in certain fantasy movies, are dead or alive. Marxism was supposedly dead; it had disappeared within global geopolitical space along with its Stalinist and Soviet version, and was electorally and socially vanquished in the West. However, the simple creed of historical materialism, the uprising of the oppressed as a mechanical consequence of structural class antagonism, is still alive, and is increasingly confirmed with each delocalization and each deregulation. Those who carry it and experience it daily are still here, and the systemic social conflict of capital against labor is more intense than ever: the violence of work, the unprecedented gap between the 1% and the 99%, and the brutality of North-South relations complicated by the rapid rise of a few countries and the migratory consequences of the great pauperization of others. These are not old leftovers from the 1960s, but the pure timeliness of today, be it with a hint of the Nietzschean untimely. We can recall the beautiful late interview given by the French writer Marguerite Duras, who, like the heroine of the film *Goodbye Lenin* waking up from a long coma in 1989, expressed mourning for the collective in the face of the "velvet" revolutions; in inimitable terms, Duras stated that shared grieving for a communal politics would henceforth be the only thing that held us together. After ten years of hysterical anticommunism during which time she was barking alongside activist Atlanticists, Duras suddenly understood that the discourses of the end that circulated everywhere (the end of communism, the end of social change, etc.) were robbing the people of that immense trust that had been granted them for nearly two centuries. It was as if the working-class person who protested weekly, or the precarious laborer on the social margins, was suddenly responsible before History for that mafia-like abomination called "communism" that the whole Eastern Bloc was finally shaking off. From then on, for Duras, the only "community would be the community of that doubt, of that unshakeable grieving"[3]—as if sharing the loss might reconstruct the lost object. In any case, loss, melancholy, remorse, and regret were all that was left for those who refused to renege on their left-ist, socialist, or Marxist commitments. The 1990s was a decade of ghosts.

But the middle of that spectral decade would see the awakening of social critique and of actual protests, from Mexico to Korea, and to the banks of the Seine. In France, thinkers who were little known at the time such as Jacques Rancière or Pierre Bourdieu would, despite themselves, become guides for renewed social conscience. Other thinkers would provide a bridge between the melancholic tradition of the extreme Left and the current protests. In the French elections of

1997–98, Trotskyist parties received unprecedented support, collectively tallying more than 10% of the vote. This was the time when nonprofits, new activist movements, and specific battlegrounds (for the unemployed, illegal immigrants, housing, etc.) were mushrooming throughout Europe. In the United States, parallel to the rise of identity politics and of minority struggles, the alter-globalization movement (a new transversal social movement with global aims) emerged in 1999 during the Seattle countersummit against the World Trade Organization. But this relative renewal—this multiplication of struggles and of micropolitics that both Mao Zedong and Michel Foucault would have considered powerful, decisive strategies to besiege the Enemy—would be viewed negatively by the classical Left from the 1990s onward as a "Balkanization" of struggles and a selfish explosion of excessively pluralist left-wing parties, when it was actually a fabulous renewal. For the last twenty years, lessons have been coming in from Latin America (where indigenous struggles and socialism have worked hand in hand, from the Chiapas region held by the Zapatistas to the high plateaus of Bolivia), Europe (where civil society and the world of nonprofits have often led more radical actions than the established leftist parties), and the Arab world (where, before this victory was stolen, the people succeeded in toppling dictators who'd been impossible to budge, giving the lie to the prejudices of White House consultants on Islam who claimed the Muslim social world was incapable of democratic uprising). Of course, from LGBTQ protests to the Arab Spring, situations and motivations are radically different. But this multiplication of causes and sites of mobilization is good news. If, in the short term, it accelerates the split with the establishment Left and intensifies the cultural divides internal to leftists, in the long term it also renews leftists' language and those they seek to address. The establishment Left must expand beyond notions of the state and of the nation to encompass the local community and intermediary bodies. As for leftists, they are no longer simply salaried workers or the electorate in need of reassurance, but also precarious workers, the long-term unemployed, women, homosexuals, migrants, religious or cultural minorities, and all of those who suffer from desocialization. In sum, the Left must reach out to all of the margins now that the working class is no longer the alpha and the omega of the social movement.

In terms of the political Left, which is the other aspect of the problem, let us look closely at the stages of its disappearance, via its collusion with the macrostructures of power. First came the experience of power, and its "long remorse" for the reformist, managerial, "realist" left.[4] Not only did the "yacht people" who had fled France after Mitterand's election in 1981 quickly return, and the most progressive US presidents Lyndon B. Johnson and Jimmy Carter not impose a New Deal to economic powers in the United States, but in all countries this shift in power was soon to be voted in by the elite. It turned out that the financial markets, the conservative bourgeoisies, the great fortunes, and the military powers preferred to have center-left personalities in power for the good of the neoliberal order and to keep the streets quiet. To serve their interests, Gerhard Schröder in Germany, Bill Clinton in the United States, and Tony Blair in Great Britain were deemed more efficient than their right-wing predecessors Helmut Kohl, Ronald Reagan, and Margaret Thatcher. They were more zealous in their dismantling of labor rights and of the welfare state via parliaments and "modern" union negotiations. It began in France with François Mitterand and in Spain with Felipe González. Their "socialist" governments, beginning before the mid-1980s, would place the administrative and expenditure-planning state in the service of the market economy by encouraging the circulation of capital, turning their countries into dynamic financial centers, and adjusting laws and minds to economic globalization. They implemented the monetary policies and the budgetary rigor required for the creation of the economic

European Union, and extolled business creation and technological progress as solutions to the economic crisis. This period saw the shift from a sovereign, protective, and redistributive state to a speculative and securitarian state that would orchestrate great international economic maneuvers and reinforce the soft surveillance of all by all. The state of grace of the early Mitterand years and of the Movida movement in post-Franco Spain was short-lived; unfortunately, the hangover would turn out to be more long-term. Such an evolution was not inscribed in the initial project of the European Community (1957), but precise decisions and options would move it in that direction—for example, the negotiations between Kohl and Mitterand in the early 1980s that would be endorsed by the 1992 referendum on the Maastricht Treaty. Faced with the economic crisis and the intensification of competition with Asian countries and with the United States, Europe (or its ruling class), rather than reinforce its redistributive and mixed economic model put in place at the end of the Second World War, openly chose to become the leader of global neoliberalism.

The Third Way played a key role in this neoliberal turn by imposing what Tony Blair coined New Public Management. It applied the managerial norms of the private sector to the state, to public institutions, and to companies—that is, reduced job security, the contractualization of employment, performance targets, continuous evaluation, the replacement of collegiality with "human resources," and individualization and responsibilization at all levels. More recently, one or two just, consensual causes have been added to try to redeem the cynicism of the new capitalism: a budding environmental awareness (with advertising campaigns and legislative measures to manage polluters though a "polluter pays" principle) and a zest of social philanthropy (by way of the supposed "social responsibility of companies" that engage in tax-exempt philanthropy, public-private partnerships, finance nonprofits, etc.) The only "social responsibility" of companies, however, is to profit, nothing else, as the neoliberal economist Milton Friedman used to say, somewhat brutally. But those two little extra touches also play the part of channeling ecological fear and social gloom in the right direction of maintaining the system. The idea is to move toward "green" capitalism, with its new lucrative niches, on one hand, and toward a charitable and socially responsible capitalism, on the other—a capitalism of moderation, for those fans of oxymora. In any case, the protective function of staving away catastrophe or poverty that had belonged to the state since the beginning of the modern era was progressively transferred to businesses and charitable organizations.

The change in France was less blatant than what has been occurring in the United States, where the so-called "nonprofit" sector of the economy had existed since the end of the nineteenth century, developed via the philanthropic initiatives of major industry and banking barons such as Andrew Carnegie and J. P. Morgan. This sector accounts for 7 to 9 percent of the United States's GDP, and possesses great stability due to fiscal measures and a tradition of volunteer work. Many economists argue that the development of a nonprofit sector at the heart of all national economies should be encouraged so as to have a pocket of activity that is less subject to the vicissitudes of the market—but also to encourage the privatization of the state, what some also call the "humanitarianizing" of the state when it promotes and finances the activity of NGOs and nonprofits.[5] This is what the official Left defended and put in place everywhere during the last quarter of the twentieth century. In the end, the political Left is now caught in a bind between a splintered extreme Left mourning its promises and rallying cries, and a managerial Left that has lost all inhibitions, outdoing the Right on the terrain of neoliberalism. The result is a general "impoten-tizing," to speak like Félix Guattari, both for left-wing sentiment and for its actual resources. These stages have led to the disappearance of the Left, whether it has become a melancholic refuge or simply a notion that has vanished from "real" politics. Consequently, the managerial Left will continually be accused of no longer being on the left, whereas those who accuse it of this treachery (the extreme Left) will be accused of being either soft utopians or rigid apologists of nostalgia. It is always the same logic of separation and resentment, this time in favor of the established order.

However, on that left-hand side of reality, several new proposals have appeared while the world was shifting to the right. These have offered reflexes for political survival and provisional answers to economic cynicism and moral conservatism, to the withdrawal around national values as well as to the new jihadist fascism. For the new shift to the right is all of these things. And indeed, we have recently witnessed a gradual yet decisive awakening and an internal mutation of the emancipatory project, although we still do not understand these events fully. If there is to be a possible transformation of the idea and the practice of "the Left," it relies on an alliance that is still to come, an alliance that is tactical and delicate because it goes against the history of the Left, the alliance between the unitary social project of sociopolitical change from the base up and the question of minorities in their irreducible plurality—or, in other words, between what Deleuze and Guattari called macropolitics, referring to social combat, and all of the micropolitics of daily secession and dissident subjectivity. There is a series of identities—ethnic, religious, sexual, social, and cultural—that function like Russian nesting dolls and which we all share in, even those among us, white men, who can least claim minority status. This segmentation of identity had long been opposed to the very idea of the Left: it is based on essences, received facts which could only be changed with difficulty (just as you cannot change the color of your skin or ancient, age-old hatred) and which were supposedly incompatible with the constructionism and unitary quality of the Left. We were simply what our economic situation and our social position had made of us, and we had to come together to change these. But today, subjectification takes place through identity, identification, and the religious or cultural interface of a relation to the world that it overcodes, even if that kind of identity is strategic, or always plural. In other words, what needs to be transformed, foregrounded, and recognized is no longer simply our socioeconomic condition to the exclusion of everything else, but also, *inseparably*, each of our subjective conditions: the condition of all women under an unscathed sexism, the status of provincials under state centralism, the position of precarious workers at the twilight of the salary system, the continuing erasure of transsexuals under state gender categories, and, on a global scale, the very deeply entrenched colonial racism affecting people of color, or the situation of Muslim citizens in this era of the horrors of the Islamic State and of antiveil laws. Here, *perhaps primarily*, is where social affect and the immediate social sentiment now lie. A unitary social struggle and the conditions of minorities must move forward hand in hand. This is what is required for the survival and the renewal of the old emancipative project. And it leads to results when both parts can tactically align. This has been the lesson of Latin America over the past twenty years, beyond the single cult example of the Zapatista revolution. Despite deceptions and wrongdoings, it is the only place in the world where the Left has conceptually reinvented itself and has gained access to power via democratic means—for the most part—without playing the game of the economic elites and of financial globalization as it had in Europe, at least at the beginning.

My goal is not to gloss over the failures or betrayals of Evo Morales in Bolivia or Rafael Correa in Ecuador, or to forget the tensions of the Chavez system in Venezuela, but to look at the rare recent experiences that were able to link socioeconomic struggle and multicultural and identity issues with the question of ecology. The Bolivarian lesson lies in that triple articulation. Because the institutional devastation of the classical Left—the weakening of unions and parties, the discrediting of the great collectives—has left a wasteland in its wake. And on that wasteland, a true emancipatory project can only spread if it is based on actual subjectivities and existential conditions—that is to say, if it takes into account the affiliations of identity via a tactical approach, as in the post-colonial theorist Gayatri Spivak's expression "strategic essentialism."[6] In certain circumstances, to foreground a cultural or religious affiliation makes it possible to escape oppression, and at the same time to rally a community and to summon a world. Choosing to wear the veil, rather than implying that women are victims of their fathers' and brothers' oppression, can be a way to free oneself from religious family injunctions as well as from the opposing directives of pornographic capitalism. That is also strategic essentialism: a single veil for a double whammy.

3. Reconciling Equality and Difference

But more profound than this, however, is the fact that over the course of a few years the rhetorical Left—the left that power has used to drape over itself, or that speaks at high-profile conventions—has swapped social equality for diversity, and has traded the class struggle, deemed a lost cause, for the condemnation of discrimination, as this is better suited to the conformism of the media and to the ferment of social networks. The issue, however, is how to reconcile and forge subjective and social struggles into a single movement. Let's look back on the awakening of emancipative forces after twenty years of neoliberal steamrolling. There have already been moves made in this direction, although the path that lies ahead is still long. One of the inaugural dates here is the sudden irruption of Zapatismo onto the global public scene on January 1st, 1994, with the local insurrection and the symbolic marches on Mexico by Subcomandante Marcos and his resistance fighters from Chiapas. This heterogeneous movement brought together expropriated indigenous people from the Mexican Southwest within a collectivist project that was open to the rest of the population. European or American intellectuals have taken this as an inaugural event: see, for example, the book by John Holloway, an Irish sociologist living in Mexico, emblematically entitled *Change the World Without Taking Power.*[7] Holloway claims that the establishment of autonomy in the Chiapas communities, after the final failure of negotiations with the Mexican government in 2001, was the most advanced experience of collective emancipation and complete self-government of the end of the century—and, no doubt, we could add, of all modern history including the Russian Soviets of

1917, the Hungarian councilists of 1919, and the Spanish republicans of 1936–39. The thousands of assemblies of the Paris Commune in 1871 were much shorter-lived than has been the Zapatista adventure. The "rebel Zapatista autonomous communities" are seen as the site of a pact between identitarian *indigenismo* and radical socialism, but also between traditional ecology (or ecosophy) and anticolonial resistance, and between antipatriarchal struggle and the fight against neoliberalism. In their own way, these Zapatista communities, even when they are poor and isolated, reconcile identity and the common—bridging the daily, deep-rooted micropolitical level and the transversal level of concrete communist universalism—and therefore encourage political emancipation at all levels, despite the fact that confrontation with the powers that be did not occur directly, and that the Federal Mexican administration maintains a grip on the actual autonomy of the Chiapas region. In any case, if social change can once again come about, it will occur through different avenues than those that Lenin had conceived of (that is, by taking up arms and seizing power)—even if, in the face of powerful opposing interests, it is hard to foresee for now how this new emancipatory horizon can spread widely if not through insurrection and the actual seizing of power, as some have argued, being that the electoral process is held in the hands of the dominant classes, populist catharsis, and the dictatorship of the majority. Can we really change the world or real life for everyone without taking political and economic power? That was the large question mark floating above the planet at the turn of the millennium. For some, the way forward was to transform minds and ways of being through new lateral solidarities, online media, and the principles of intellectual equality and collective intelligence. For those who were wary of surges of disempowerment or a politics that had its head in the clouds, the solution was instead the creation of organized alternative communities, the secession of entire neighborhoods in large cities and in remote rural areas, a kind of separatism that accepted its frontal opposition to power, not aiming to seize it but instead to constantly defy it, and to "depose" it by all possible means and stratagems. Indeed, according to one of its theoreticians, this new emancipative power saw itself as a destituent rather than a constituent power.

To return to the Zapatista uprising, it inaugurated a series of several social-indigenous experiments in Latin America, including the active multiculturalism of Lula's Workers' Party in Brazil in its early days. We know the slip-ups of those neo-Bolivarian movements beginning with Hugo Chavez's Bona-partism in Venezuela, but overall Latin America has had the merit of tracing a new, promising path.

And beyond the Bolivarian dream, the awakening of emancipatory politics was global, with the December 1995 strikes in France and the new social movements that were invented in their wake, and with the emergence of the alter-globalization movement just prior to the year 2000. In a few months, activist groups formed around the defense of precarious workers, other workers, and indebted students, and autonomous ecologists appeared in public space and in the headlines of media such as Reclaim the Streets or Direct Action Network. This alter-globalization era would last five years. A number of countersummits were held and were extremely agitated: Genoa in Italy in 2001, where a young protester died; or the European summit held in Nice … After 2001, the movement itself would suffer from the "clash of civilizations" doctrine and the police state put in place after the September 11 attacks. But it would also fall prey to an internal split that was often orchestrated by the police and pitted a radical minority (the "black bloc" and other rioters) against a more established pacifist majority that came together every year for the World Social Forum initially held in Porto Alegre, Brazil. The gap would progressively widen between an offensive avant-garde that had no representatives and was decried by the media and other pontificators, and a majority movement that was more invested in reflexive indignation and a kind of self-righteousness. Incidentally, the primary alter-globalization slogan, "Another World Is Possible," took up the eschatological idea according to which everything would finally be better in the future, after the great devastation. This faith in better tomorrows and this way to postpone effective action until the future seemed to fall more into line with Christian teleology or with the propaganda of revolutionary bureaucracies. In any case, it had little to do with the force of insurrection in its own right. In a nutshell, the idea was to believe in tomorrow because we couldn't do much to change the world today.

Of course, this new activist generation is too recent and varied, enriched by its interwoven causes, to be reduced to such a slogan. It is teeming with groups and subgroups, with long-winded and with more active elements, with new knowledge and improbable causes. On the larger chronological level, the alter-globalization era that straddled the new millennium occupies an important place. From the perspective of political efficacy, two important innovations occurred during those years, seen in events from the uprising of the Zapatistas to the struggles for undocumented immigrants or for decent housing. First was the tight link, mentioned previously, between social struggles and micropolitical questions or pride in identity. Second was the radical pragmatism of operational modes. None of these groups was transversal and unitary; each was constituted around a specific cause, a precise oppression, and the effective means that had to be invented or tried out to combat it. This was how these struggles were able to immediately elude the stigma that now affects general politics and totalizing approaches—whether they are Marxist or Hegelian, or whether they concern the communist class struggle or the abstract universalism of the Republic. The new generations no longer believe in these circular lines of reasoning with no concrete anchor. And the more specific the cause, the more the means become daring, obstinate, and diehard. Look at the communities of autonomous ecologists that have set themselves up in the countryside: the squatters in Western France who are protesting an airport, the people at Standing Rock Reservation working to stop a giant pipeline running through their lands, the groups who are experienced in the wildcat and long-lasting requisitioning of buildings in upperclass neighborhoods, people fighting for the defense of illegal immigrants, the masked performances of the Génération Précaire (Precarious Generation) collective condemning the impoverishment of internships, or the hacktivist pirating of databanks. And if by chance a common context comes along, groups and specific causes can join forces, united by a common enemy, solidary tactics, and a shared counterhegemonic vision.

The second half of the 1990s was indeed a moment of social awakening, but the September 11 attacks, interpreted by the global elites as a deep paradigm shift, justified bringing to a sudden standstill this vague and still timid awakening of resistance. Suddenly, there were more urgent questions on the horizon: the War on Terror, the clash of civilizations, the global religious turn ... The generalized torpor that followed was astounding. In the United States, social movements and critical intellectuals suddenly entered into a voluntary phase of self-criticism and of shuttering of activity. With very few exceptions, everyone walled themselves off into contrite silence. From the anticapitalist form of libertarian anarchism to what was left of dissident leftism and collectivism in the United States, and especially to the sexual or ethnic identity politics that had been very active on college campuses, everyone sank into general torpor and shame after September 11, 2001. This was very striking in the university, which is usually a bubble cut off from the rest of the world in which all kinds of storms can occur without overflowing into real society, and where discourse can be that much more impassioned. But this time, a good part of the critical academic world passed judgment on itself. Not only were the questions of decentering the white man, deposing the West, or invoking a queer or postcolonial revolution no longer on the table, but many of those who had been proclaiming such injunctions engaged in acts of contrition, wondering if their irresponsibility or their hyperbole hadn't contributed to the fall of the Twin Towers! In any case, many toed the line in September 2001 and sometimes became conservative. Some argued that attacking the West for its imperialism, its machismo, and its racism had paved the way for Al-Qaeda. This gave great importance to the performative power of academic speech. It also forgot to distinguish authors (and their ideas) from the political uses that can be made of them: Nietzsche was not a Hitlerian, and Foucault was not a Maoist just because Maoist China praised his critique of Western liberalism. In any case, for two or three years an appalling torpor reigned in the academy as well as in the media.

And this standstill would last for a long time. Starting with the American occupation of Iraq in 2004, a large antiwar movement would form in the United States with millions of protesters, notably in New York and Washington. But the civilizational blackmail had more lasting effects, with its delusional cultural enemy, and the torpor that followed September 11 had important consequences on people's minds. It would take no less than ten years

for the shaming of social movements and for
academic self-critique to fade, and for people once
again to dare to stand up directly against the
dominant order. The media, which always con-
forms to the dominant ideology, would provide
the best illustration, reopening their pages and
their screens to social injustice after a decade
during which they'd been docilely won over to the
theories of Samuel Huntington. We could even say
that once the "clash of civilizations" fable had been
pushed to the side, the beginning of the social
awakening triggered by the alter-globalization
movement of the 1990s could finally resume,
spread, and open onto new transversal movements,
both civic and more offensive: the Indignados at
the Puerta del Sol in Spain in 2012–13, Occupy
Wall Street in New York and then in the rest of
North America in 2011–12, the mislabeled "Arab
Spring" uprisings at the end of 2010, or, more
recently, the heated French Social Spring of 2016.
There is an underground continuity, which must
absolutely be reestablished, between the social
forums or counterforums of the end of the century
and the converging forms of popular protest that
have recently appeared twelve years later.

Just as the War on Terror had usefully shifted
attention away from the new social struggles at the
time, the attacks by the Islamic State in Europe
in 2015–17 and the state of emergency that was

instituted in France (the hardest-hit country) as a response offered convenient, literally diabolical (in the Greek sense of *diabolos*, to separate) diversions from the global social struggle that was in the process of being reborn. Bin Laden's henchmen—just like the ISIS recruits of today, issues of migration or, the increasingly tragic Israeli-Palestinian situation—function as so many expedient red flags or evil amulets that can easily be brandished as soon as people start to mobilize in a more transversal way to defend an economic or social right that some spurious or even criminal legislation is trying to remove. Take, for example, the Patriot Act and banking deregulation under George W. Bush, or the militarized state of emergency and the neoliberal El Khomri law in France under François Hollande. And yet, despite all that, the social movement is alive and well everywhere in the world, more or less durable following the great protests of the beginning of the decade, or even encouraged by austerity measures and ballooning security politics that throw the new victims of economic precarization into its arms. And it is not slackening. In a few years, we've just seen great labor wars in South Korea, resistance movements against industrial displacements in China (about which we know only very little), strong social mobilization in Southern Europe (Spain, Italy, Greece) against the austerity politics coming out of

Brussels, Occupy Wall Street in more than a thousand North American cities, and a Latin America that continues as best it can to blend socialism and *indigenismo*. Once again, in this panorama of global social awakening we can include the "Arab Spring" protests of 2011–12 in a key role, for even if they partook of a different logic to some degree, they saw the creation and perpetuation of a genuine social movement that, before the return of the Islamists or of the military juntas, put an end to dictatorships that had been felt to be irremovable.

Of course, these recent, sporadic, and more or less mediatized resistance movements each have their particular logic and context. Their symbolic interconnection—projected on a large screen via Skype, either in the middle of Syntagma Square in Athens, Greece, or in the first Occupy Wall Street camp in lower Manhattan—does not make them into a united front, far from it. But there are nonetheless structural and systemic causes of the temporal convergence of these phenomena, and they share the same direct historical trigger—the 2008–9 financial crisis, which was partly covered up, or made irreversible, by the state-funded bailout of banks and insurance giants. This muffled crisis destabilized developing countries through a ricochet effect and pushed large swaths of the populations of so-called rich countries into poverty. It therefore had very direct sociopolitical effects, attested by the scale of the uprisings in the years that followed. These might not be coordinated between themselves, but they are at least stimulated, and at times galvanized, by the consciousness they have of each other via references on blogs or social networks, and even in a semi-institutional way through social forums or by means of certain intellectuals. Between them, there is of course no direct political cooperation or strategy of unification, but they make many references to one another, invoke the most distant examples and offer active solidarity to each other whenever they can. The instigators of the Nuit Debout movement in Paris made reference to the campers of the Puerta del Sol, although they did not explicitly align themselves with them. The latter had invoked the achievements of the Occupy Wall Street movement the previous fall, which had itself made an explicit link with the alter-globalists of the previous decade. And all of them referred back to the Zapatistas in Chiapas and to the Tunisian revolution of 2011 … Being inscribed in the same lineage and in the same global space of struggle does not, of course, make for an organized movement, but this is already the sketch of a global common consciousness.

The question remains of the electoral institutionalization of these movements. We are thinking of Podemos in Spain and Syriza in Greece, two political forces carried by powerful social movements that won decisive victories at the ballot box but whose results afterward were not what their supporters had expected. Both of these movements raise a delicate and burning issue to which we do not have any answers: at what moment and in what conditions can we move from the refusal of representation to the necessity, even if it is only tactical, of representing those concerned more largely, and even of potentially representing everyone? In other words, how do you move from systematic blockage to leading the system without compromising your commitments? And what could be the process to institutionalize a lateral, spontaneous, and radical movement that refuses, a priori, traditional political representation? How can it establish rules and lead an autonomous policy? For, once this kind of movement gains a critical mass, with a national mobilization and a majority of public opinion in its favor, it finds itself at the gates of power, with elections within its reach. It must then institutionalize its procedures, its program, and its representatives before gaining access to power, as it happened in Greece and somewhat in Spain. And there, without institutional change, the experience of power quickly becomes problematic, forcing these movements to enter into a series of negotiations and compromises that jeopardize their principles. During the summer of 2015, the Greek prime minister Alexis Tsipras was forced into a semiausterity compromise with Europe; and the following year, Podemos, which won mayoral races in Barcelona and Madrid, had to lower the hopes of general reform inherited from the Puerta del Sol. Of course, these city councils are delaying the evacuation of squats and increasing cultural budgets or funding for refugees, but without a more extensive modification of the rules of the game. For everything else, they have no other choice than to promote the implantation of foreign companies and the investment logics that dominate elsewhere.

Today, this question of institutionalization and of its risks lies at the core of the problem. From a multiparty Europe, where the great parties are in crisis, to a bipartisan America, where the Trump opposition has not yet found an institutional translation, should we completely circumvent elections and act in other ways, or should we run for electoral office hoping to change what we will be able to change? The question of the institution is a complex theoretical one, and was masterfully exposed in Cornelius Castoriadis's book *The Imaginary Institution of Society*.[8] For the imagination is a social force unto itself, and a social movement is something more than an abstract idea, a soft utopia, or a rhetorical catharsis once it becomes established by naming itself or ensuring the durability of its procedures—in sum, once it attempts to *constitute itself*. The small country of Tunisia is the hero of the moment, proof that a process of collective constitution does not always get nipped in the bud. While Egypt was falling into the hands of the army and Libya and Syria were descending into chaos, Tunisia held on after having ousted its dictator, Ben Ali, inaugurating a long and cumbersome constitutional process from below—at the price of an ungovernable country and an aggravated economic situation, and against the background of the rise of the Islamist party Ennahdha and pressure from Western countries. These were the memorable stakes of the 1792 constitution during the French Revolution: the constitution of a commons, an effective political body that was national or even larger, based on an open, interminable discussion about the common rules that would enable the institution of a just distribution of economic wealth, of the fruits of labor, of a common cultural heritage, and of inherited ideas. In any case, it seems that there are many pertinent lessons coming from the South for us children of the North, lessons from the autonomous inhabitants of the Exarcheia neighborhood in Athens, or from the Tunisian or Zapatista social forces leading fragile processes of constitution.

4. The Specter of the People

In both cases, whether in a disenchanted North or a remobilized South, a gap remains between activist youth who are often either students or educated, and the more oppressed, more invisible populations. The objective conditions for a more general uprising will be met once this gap is closed. There is the neoliberal segmentation of urban space between touristic urban centers and social housing projects, lawless enclaves, and areas under excessive close surveillance. In the same way as European budgetary policies led to leaving entire neighborhoods in Southern European cities or isolated rural areas to fend for themselves, the "structural adjustments" of the IMF accelerated the rift in developing countries between luxury real-estate complexes and uncontrolled slums (in Latin American megalopolises and soon in Africa), just as housing-project policies created the spatial segregation operative in France between cities and suburban neighborhoods, those zones of exclusion. In all of these cases we have populations disconnected from political representation and even from any nonlocal social movement, partially self-organized, reduced to strategies of collective survival at best and to intercommunity wars or identitarian compensation at worst. But we cannot simply decree the junction of urban social struggles with these enclaves of ghettoized neighborhoods or semideserted rural areas. And in fact, this junction is struggling to cement itself. Leninists believed that the revolutionary social movement could not be unleashed by the subalterns at the base of the ladder of oppression, but rather by somewhat less disadvantaged classes, whose own consciousness could be raised by their own degree of freedom, and who would be joined, when the time came, by the available lumpenproletariat. On the contrary, radical postcolonial thinkers such as the Indian Dipesh Chakrabarty, today, or C. L. R. James, yesterday, believe that only those who have absolutely nothing to lose, in the rivalry between the North and the South as well as in their own social structure, can spearhead the social offensives to come. It is difficult to generalize here, but it would be better, at a minimum, to stop accusing the social movement of being disjointed from abandoned neighborhoods, inner-city ghettoes, or post-colonial suburbs.

Because they have never been to these places, the self-righteous among the official Left, whose indignation is mostly moral or strategic, and the white conservatives, with their dark visions, have a hard time imagining that people might live more intensely where the value of life is under threat. People live there too, of course. People create and refuse there, laugh and love there. And perhaps they don't even die or suffer there more than elsewhere. It's easy to go there and see; it's just next-door. One of the most interesting aspects of the contemporary social movement foregrounded by young theorists is an unprecedented concern for the life and the joy—the "cheerful disposition," as Spinoza would say—at the heart of the worst, or simply within the disaster of the ordinary, in the most underprivileged projects, in the "jungle" of migrants at the borders of Europe, or in the abandoned neighborhoods of American megalopolises. This well-intentioned view is not moral, as it were.

For we must balance the direct, intersubjective violence that is often more perceptible in these places with the systemic violence that is less visible but much more constraining and which overdetermines everyone's life, including the lives of those who live in nice residential neighborhoods. The humanitarian vision of all of these derogatory zones, defined by urgency and survival, has often turned them into spaces that belong more to fantasy than to reality. Daily life there has become inconceivable. As Gilles Deleuze wrote in his 1976 pamphlet against the Nouveaux Philosophes, their "morbid martyrology" had pulled them away from the self-evident facts of life. They had forgotten that when you are closest to the danger of death, you are also closest to the power of life.[9] Of course, we must be careful not to romanticize misery into fairy tales of ingenuity, but those who were crazy enough to insist on going out dancing in Beirut nightclubs before the end of the terrible Lebanese civil war demonstrated this well enough. That city, which has been destroyed over and over again, had and still has the wildest, most electric nightlife in the Middle East, with its bullet-riddled walls and its nightclubs improvised in garages … There is something like an invisible fringe, an adjoining, nondialectical link between the danger of death and the power of life, between joy and despair, between devastation and socialization. Whiny discourse has disastrous effects, because it is performative and produces in those who listen to it the sad passion that it attributes to these lives and to these places. In the same way, on the other side, the external signs of a successful life under the neoliberal regime of people who belong to the majority and have a comfortable income can hide situations of great sexual, psychic, or emotional misery (as chronicled since the end of the twentieth century in the novels of Michel Houellebecq or Russell Banks). To recall the power of life of these banished zones is also to oppose this power to the powers of death, to the miserable orgy of death of those few lost souls who decided one day to blow themselves up in a concert hall or an airport terminal.

The dominant economism, from the liberals in power to orthodox Marxists, has a hard time taking all of this into account. This is also where the biopolitical horizon changes the playing field, for it takes charge of what traditional revolutionaries did not know or forgot on purpose. We cannot simply attack social and economic misery; we must also eradicate psychic, spiritual, and sexual misery, all of which arise in part from the same logic. But our compartmentalized, isolated, hyperconnected lives don't make the task easy—far from it, since they widen the spectrum of promises and deceptions and intensify our divisions, all that *schiz* that makes up the folly and the bliss of the capitalist "dream" (that consubstantial link between capitalism and schizophrenia established by Deleuze and Guattari). Doomed to systemic uncertainty and to technological prostheses, individual existence is more than ever a collection of Russian nesting dolls, an arrangement of strata and positions in which each element does not follow an evolution that parallels the others.

The same is true of the elitist critique of the cultural industry, which elitism was already the great Theodor Adorno's error in the 1950s. For if the notion of a counterculture is somewhat unwieldy, it points to creative practices that are more linked to forms of life than in popular or high culture. Behind the great neoliberal shift or in its interstices, the 1980s and 1990s also produced their own countercultures: punk and disco, then the electro and dance music of the early rave scene, or the gangsta-rap scene before the major American labels got involved. A traditional Marxist might try to see in this a superstructural diversion in the field of culture, of political power-lessness and economic oppression, and thus understand these forms as reactionary musical productions keeping us away from social struggle. Yet these were not simply aesthetic crystallizations of powerlessness, but also mute forms continuing the sociopolitical uprising in the only place where it could still occur. This was no longer in the elec-toral process or in the traditional social movement, but in bodily countercultures: music and dance, drawing and alternative "sports," in skate parks or by scaling buildings or structures to tag. These were ways to become one on the ruins of the col-lective body, through the trance of the first "teknivals" or the irony of the new amateur singers. Today, it is more important than ever to attentively observe these more or less spontaneous countercultural forms that were invented on the Internet or at the corner bar. Because that is where a new distribution of the sensible is being invented, an unprecedented allocation of perceptions that can displace the gaze, reactivate common synesthe-sia, and eventually make a social uprising possible, a more literal uprising of the same bodies. The early 1990s was the lowest point of the social movement in Europe and in North America, and yet this was when twenty-year-olds met in abandoned warehouses from Manchester to Detroit to the fields of Southwest France to dance until exhaustion under the effects of psychotropic drugs, before the police outlawed these movements and major labels took over their music. From a certain point of view, the political body is also the common body that is available to fulfill a collective desire; it is therefore also the sweating body of those young people from already twenty-five years ago. In a Balkanized, anomic, segregated, and individualized society, a certain continuity of bodies still remains, a unity of bodies in time, bodies that dance one moment and burn cars or put up barricades the next. Here is another image of this possible junction, in both directions: the image of people from the hood who come dance in front of the Occupy Wall Street tents or listen to an amateur dub musician or to more political rap songs during the impromptu concerts of Nuit Debout on the Place de la République in Paris, and the symmetrical image of underground shows during which young middle-class kids set foot in the hood for the first time.

For all of these reasons, we have to stop fantasizing about the resistance, neither projecting it into the future, after the eureka moment that will activate all of us, nor into the past, where the term "resistance," which is so European, has been stuck for the last seventy-five years, caught between the ghosts of Nazism and its rare heroic enemies. It would be better to demystify the resistance, to make it less totalizing, to cobble it together, to miniaturize it and anchor it in the present where it is permanent. It is an inexplicable tangle of refusals, perplexities, skepticism, and effective gestures that escape the dominant order, whether this means pirating videos, hijacking slogans, producing your own food, expressing your disagreement in verse form, or simply teaching or writing something other than what was asked of you. Recipes for survival, DIY tips, hacking instructions, ways to dodge paying for public transportation, unexpected jokes, solidarity that was never required, nonconforming life choices: it is through such tricks and ruses that the resistance always already exists, that it cannot not exist, and that it has already begun to defy, everywhere and in every instant, that dominant socioeconomic order to which some more narrow-minded people despair of ever finding an "alternative." This alternative exists. It takes a thousand microscopic forms. It is hardheaded. It is becoming generalized, tangled up, and also more refined.

We are just a step away from an active and global collective resistance, and from an irreversible process, but it is a very large step. A few major "junctions" need to occur: the global junction between the North and the South, the one between the suburbs and the inner cities, the one between a unitary movement and micropolitical struggles, or between rights and bodies. We must all, of course, at our own level, take care that the globalized chaos that the planet has inherited after fifty years of counterrevolution favors neither crazy theocrats nor fascistic patriots—that is, neither the Islamic State nor the Donald Trumps of every country. There remains, of course, the decisive nudge of "objective circumstances," when one more crisis, one lie too many, or one more meaningless death could spark off a situation that seemed stuck. The time that goes by without any of the recent social movements being able to last or to finally crystallize the discontent is a time that is nonetheless in their favor. A half century of crimes, of reforms, and of guile will have been necessary to establish the securitarian neoliberal regime that is in place today, a regime that in some respects seems already obsolete. It will not be toppled in a day or in a year, but once all the thresholds of the tolerable have been crossed. When the uprising will occur is now just a question of time. And the new form it will take, a form that must be invented, is just a question of imagination. Luckily, many people everywhere are working toward this, taking the time they need. Just like that slogan that activists in the 1990s painted onto the front of a large investment bank, "You Have the Money, but We Have the Time."

Notes

Introduction

1. "If the West calls someone a dictator, in my view that is a good thing," Erdogan stated on Nov. 22, 2016 at the opening ceremony of the Organization of Islamic Cooperation (quoted in http://www.al-monitor.com/pulse/originals/2016/12/turkey-erdo-gan-being-labeled-as-dictator-is-compliment.html).

2. See Ron Norland, "Authoritarian Leaders Greet Trump as One of Their Own," *New York Times*, Feb. 1, 2017, https://www.nytimes.com/ 2017/02/01/world/asia/donald-trump-vladimir-putin-rodri-go-dutert-kim-jong-un.html?emc=edit_ae_20170201&nl=todaysheadlines-asia&nlid=67293453&_r=1.

1. A Counterrevolution in Three Parts

1. Alain Bertho, *Anthropologie du présent* [Anthropology of the Present], https://berthoalain.com/documents/.

2. Michel de Certeau, *The Practice of Everyday Life*, transl. Steven Rendall (Berkeley, CA: University of California Press, 1984).

3. Francis Fukuyama, *The End of History and the Last Man* (New York: Free Press, 2006).

4. Gilles Châtelet, *To Live and Think Like Pigs: The Incitement of Envy and Boredom in Market Democracies*, transl. Robin Mackay, foreword Alain Badiou (New York: Sequence/Urbanomic Press, 2014).

5. Karl Marx and Friedrich Engels, *The German Ideology*, transl. C. J. Arthur (New York: International Publishers, 1970); Louis Althusser, "Ideology and Ideological State Apparatuses," in *Lenin and Philosophy, and Other Essays*, transl. Ben Brewster and Gerald Cinamon (London: NLB, 1971).

6. Samuel P. Huntington, *The Clash of Civilizations?: The Debate* (New York: Norton, 1996).

7. Naomi Klein, *The Rise of Disaster Capitalism* (London: Allen Lane, 2007).

8. See the article on the Lundi Matin website, "La guerre véritable" [The True War], https://lundi.am/La-guerre-veritable.

9. Thomas Frank, *What's the Matter with Kansas?: How Conservatives Won the Heart of America* (New York: Picador, 2005).

10. Enzo Traverso, *Le passé, modes d'emploi. Histoire, mémoire, politique* [User Manuals for the Past: History, Memory, Politics] (La Fabrique, Paris, 2005).

11. François Hartog, *Regimes of Historicity: Presentism and Experiences of Time*, trans. Saskia Brown (New York: Columbia University Press, 2015).

2. Order, Technics, Life

1. Hakim Bey, *T.A.Z.: The Temporary Autonomous Zone, Ontological Anarchy, Poetic Terrorism* (Brooklyn, NY: Autonomedia, 2003).

2. Notably Michael Hardt and Antonio Negri, *Empire* (Cambridge, Mass: Harvard University Press, 2001) and *Multitude: War and Democracy in the Age of Empire* (London: Penguin Books, 2006).

3. Yves Citton, *The Ecology of Attention*, transl. Barnaby Norman (Cambridge, UK: Polity, 2016).

4. Michel Foucault, *The Birth of Biopolitics: Lectures at the Collège De France, 1978–1979*, transl. Michel Senellart (New York: Picador, 2010).

5. Ulrich Beck, *Risk Society: Towards a New Modernity* (London: Sage, 1992).

6. Michel Foucault, *The History of Sexuality*, transl. Robert Hurley (New York: Pantheon Books, 1978).

7. A French community-based nonprofit dedicated to fighting HIV/AIDS—Transl.

8. Henry David Thoreau, *Civil Disobedience and Other Essays* (New York: Dover, 1993).

9. François Furet, Jacques Julliard, and Pierre Rosanvallon, *La République du centre: la fin de l'exception française* [The Republic of the Center: the End of the French Exception] (Paris: Calmann-Lévy, 1988).

10. Todd Gitlin, *The Twilight of Common Dreams: Why America is Wracked by Culture Wars* (New York: Metropolitan Books, 1995).

11. Herbert Marcuse, *Eros and Civilization; A Philosophical Inquiry into Freud* (London: Penguin Press, 1970); Sigmund Freud, *Civilization and Its Discontents* (London: L. & Virginia Woolf at the Hogarth Press, etc., 1903); Hannah Arendt, *On Violence* (New York: Harcourt, Brace & World, Inc., 1970).

3. Countering the Right Without Seizing Power?

1. *Time Magazine*, Sep. 5, 1977.

2. Jacques Derrida, *Specters of Marx: The State of the Debt, the Work of Mourning and the New International*, transl. Peggy Kamuf (New York: Routledge, 2006).

3. Marguerite Duras, "Marguerite Retrouvée," [Interview with Marguerite Duras] *Le Nouvel Observateur*, May 24–30, 1990.

4. Alain Bergounioux and Gérard Grunberg, *Le Long Remords du Pouvoir: le Parti Socialiste Français (1905–1992)* [The Long Remorse of Power: the French Socialist Party (1905–1992)] (Paris: Fayard, 1992).

5. The term is taken from the sociologist Didier Fassin, *La raison humanitaire. Une histoire morale du temps présent* [Humanitarian Reason: a Moral History of the Present] (Paris: Gallimard, Seuil, 2010).

6. See, notably, Gayatri Chakravorty Spivak, *Nationalism and the Imagination* (London: Seagull Books, 2010).

7. John Holloway, *Change the World Without Taking Power: The Meaning of Revolution Today* (London: Pluto, 2002).

8. Cornelius Castoriadis, *The Imaginary Institution of Society* (Cambridge, UK: Polity Press, 1987).

9. Gilles Deleuze, "On the New Philosophers and a More General Problem," transl. Bertrand Augst, *Discourse* 20, no. 3 (Fall 1998): 37–43.

ABOUT THE AUTHOR

François Cusset is Professor of American Studies at the University of Paris-Ouest Nanterre. A specialist in contemporary intellectual and political history, he is the author of *French Theory: How Foucault, Derrida, Deleuze, & Co Transformed the Intellectual Life of the United States* and *The Inverted Gaze: Queering the French Literary Classics in America.*